Come Up Higher

Part Two

by Marilyn Gool

**A 90-day devotional guide
for those who desire a deeper
relationship with God**

**Conquerors Publishing
Charlotte, North Carolina**

All scriptures have been taken from the King James Version, unless otherwise noted.

Copyright © 1996 by Marilyn Gool
All rights reserved.

Come Up Higher
Part Two
Published by Conquerors Publishing
    P.O. Box 240433
    Charlotte, NC 28224

ISBN 0-9648460-3-9

ACKNOWLEDGEMENTS

I give thanks to God first for the honor of being His vessel to bless people.

I am grateful for the support of my husband, Robyn, whose encouragement means very much to me.

I thank the Ladies of Victory staff, who also encouraged me in this project.

Special thanks to Treva Farmer, who edited the text, and Freddricka L. Allen who volunteered her time to do the typesetting.

This book belongs to

_____

I began reading Day 91 on _____

Please return to the following address:

_____

_____

INTRODUCTION

I remember the excitement I felt the day I believe the Lord said He wanted to share some things with me. He invited me to have a seat and listen. I felt led to write down the scripture I heard Him refer to, as well as the exhortation that went along with it.

This began a new thing with the Lord and me. It continued for months, before I realized this was not just for me. It did not dawn on me, for quite some time, why I was being led to write down what I was hearing.

I believe His plan was for me to write a daily devotional. This new kind of devotional has been created for those who desire a deeper relationship with God. It does not start on any particular date. Day one is the day you begin. There are four parts to this series - a total of 360 days.

I pray that your life will be greatly enriched by this book. May you be a more useful servant in God's kingdom as a result of it.

Day 91
Revelation 21:4

"And God shall wipe away all tears from their eyes; and there shall be no more death, neither sorrow, nor crying, neither shall there be any more pain: for the former things are passed away."

As we look at what God plans to do at the consummation of the ages, His will for man becomes clear. The activities of evil will cease, not because God will decide that there should be no more darkness, but because the perpetrator of evil will have been done away with forever.

Because man was given jurisdiction over the earth for a period of time, we do not see the perfect will of God in operation. Man's will plays a part. Because man yielded to Satan, Satan has brought in his wickedness.

When the time of man's dominion over the earth is complete, Jesus will reign here forever and ever. Then we will see the perfect will of God demonstrated without hindrance. Meanwhile, as we labor with God, our mission is to bring the greatest amount of liberty to humanity we can. Jesus did that while He was on the earth. As He wiped tears, reversed death, eliminated sorrow and crying, and freed people from pain, He demonstrated the will of His Father.

The God and Father of our Lord Jesus Christ is our Father. Before He left earth to return to Heaven, Jesus told His disciples He was sending them as the Father had sent Him. So let us continue the mission to bring deliverance from evil to all who want to be free.

I will be about my Father's business, setting people free from darkness, bringing light and life to all who will receive.

Day 92

I Corinthians 3:19 NIV

"For the wisdom of this world is foolishness in God's sight. As it is written: "He catches the wise in their craftiness."

We must always remember that God sees and knows far more than we do. No matter how much experience we have had or how much insight we have gained on a subject, there is One who understands better.

Men do extensive research and come up with answers. They perform scientific testing and come up with solutions. Nevertheless, they continue to change their minds, as new evidence which contradicts previous discoveries is found. Something is revealed to alter what they thought were conclusive findings.

It is most disgusting to see humans come up with "answers" that contradict God's Word. That is the ultimate stupidity. In any event, God is not moved by man's feeble attempt to show how smart or self-sufficient he is. He continues to baffle their minds, often using less educated, less skilled people who trust and rely on Him for insight. He shows what they consider foolish advice to be superior to their diligent studies.

If we want to stay ahead in life and receive the best advice, we must not rely solely on man's wisdom. God can use something foolish to humiliate those who act as though they do not need Him. God's wisdom does not always make sense to the carnal mind, but it will always be the best advice, if we want to guarantee success.

To stay ahead, let us seek God's face continually. We can avoid blunders and humiliation by submitting our intelligence to the source of all true wisdom.

I will seek God's face continually. I will receive and act on the wisdom He shares with me and continue to succeed in life.

Day 93

James 3:17 NIV

"But the wisdom that comes from Heaven is first of all pure; then peace-loving, considerate, submissive, full of mercy and good fruit; impartial and sincere."

We already know the wisdom of God will not contradict the Word of God. There are also ways we can test the source of wisdom we believe we have received. James gives us eight points to consider. Let us put them in question form.

Is it pure? This question will be settled to a great degree by measuring it through God's Word.

Does it produce peace? As much as possible, we should choose the direction that will produce a peaceful outcome. The Bible instructs us to do our best to live peaceably with everyone. Everything that is pure will not necessarily promote peace.

Will we be submissive when we do it? God respects order. If we do things that prove we are rebellious to those in authority, we have not operated in God's wisdom.

Is it full of mercy? We do not need to do everything we have a right to do. It is God's wisdom for us to show mercy. That does not necessarily mean we should allow someone to get away with wrongdoing. It does mean, however, that we should not go to the extent we could rightfully go to. This is wise, because we need very much to sow seeds in our areas of need. We all need mercy.

Does it produce good fruit? A tree is known by its fruit. We can determine the wisdom of our actions by the long-term results.

Is it impartial? We must be fair, because God is fair. That does not mean we should treat everyone the same. It just means our treatment should not vary for selfish reasons. In other words, we should not give special treatment for personal gain.

Is it sincere? Are we performing to give people a false impression of us? If we are trying to win favor by living two lives, we are certainly not representing God. He does not alter His standards for anyone. Nobody wants clean food on a dirty plate. Most people want to be ministered to by those who do what they do from their hearts.

If we would use this checklist to examine our decisions, it can save us from many blunders. We can become more and more like Jesus, if we practice operating in heavenly wisdom.

My actions will be pure, peaceable, considerate, submissive, full of mercy, impartial and sincere. They will produce good, long-term results.

Day 94
James 3:13 NIV

"Who is wise and understanding among you? Let him show it by his good life, by deeds done in humility that comes from wisdom."

As we examine ourselves to see how much wisdom we are walking in, it is good to remember that wisdom and humility are inseparable. It is totally unwise to walk in pride. It is possible to begin operating in godly wisdom and slip into earthly wisdom, when we begin to experience positive results. We can be so mindful of our need for God's help before we see success. Then as things start to go well, we can begin to lean on our own understanding. So, walking in the wisdom from above is not a one-time decision that permanently determines our state of affairs. A quality decision to walk in true wisdom is important. However, we must constantly monitor our behavior and motives to stay on the right road.

We should review our course every day and, if necessary, repent from walking in devilish or sensual wisdom. No effort needs to be made to flow with the spirit of the world, because it permeates the air around us. If we are going to walk in the spirit, we must make a conscientious effort to do so. We must depend on God, not our own strength, as we press toward our goal.

I walk in humility daily, as I continue to operate in godly wisdom. With God's help, I will remain on the right path.

Day 95
Psalm 119: 98-99

"Thou through thy commandments hast made me wiser than mine enemies: for they are ever with me. I have more understanding than all my teachers: for thy testimonies are my meditation."

The psalmist claimed that meditating God's Word increased his wisdom and understanding. He was wiser than his enemies and had more understanding than his teachers. He did nothing difficult to accomplish that. However, he had to be diligent.

We can increase our wisdom to whatever degree we desire. It depends on how much effort we are willing to put forth. Our understanding can grow if we are not lazy. Sometimes our understanding of one thing depends on our having clarity in another area. Like the psalmist, if we love wisdom, we must make meditating and studying God's Word a priority.

Let us ingest the Word at least as many times in a day as we ingest physical food. We make sure we eat to keep our bodies healthy and strong. That is a priority for us. We should consider our spiritual health and strength no less important. As a matter of fact, we need to keep in mind that good spiritual health and strength will positively affect our physical well-being.

I will give attention to the Word of God daily, at least as many times as I feed my body. I will be healthy and strong, both spiritually and physically.

Day 96
Ephesians 1:18

"The eyes of your understanding being enlightened: that ye may know what is the hope of His calling, and what the riches of the glory of His inheritance in the saints,"

Paul told the church at Ephesus that he prayed for their spiritual understanding, so they would know the hope they had been called to and the riches of the glorious inheritance Jesus had in the saints. We do not have to understand everything we act on, but understanding does help us. Sometimes, understanding will determine whether or not we act properly. Lack of understanding can cause us not to respond when we should. It can also cause us to do the wrong things. Understanding is valuable.

Jesus said in Matthew 13:19 that when a person hears the Word of the kingdom and does not understand it, the devil snatches away the Word that was sown in his heart. On the other hand, He said in the 23rd verse that the one who understands the Word will bear fruit.

Reading can help us gather knowledge. Meditation and study, combined with prayer, will produce understanding of the knowledge we obtain. Knowledge alone is not very helpful. Furthermore, it can be harmful without understanding and wisdom.

Let us seek to increase in knowledge <u>and</u> understanding. This means we should not hurriedly gather information in quantity only. We should take more time to get understanding of what we learn.

I will pray before and while I study and mediate God's Word. I will increase in knowledge and understanding and be fruitful.

Day 97
Ephesians 6:17

"And take the helmet of salvation, and the sword of the spirit, which is the Word of God."

The soldier's helmet is the piece of armor that protects his head. The skull is the part of the head which covers the brain. The brain sends messages to the entire body and gives instructions on how to function. If something goes wrong with the brain, the whole body becomes dysfunctional. Thinking processes become confused, and our effectiveness as a part of society is reduced or eliminated.

The spiritual armor of salvation protects our brains from improper spiritual thinking. If we do not see ourselves in light of the great salvation, which has been provided for us, our thinking processes become confused. Our effectiveness as a part of the army of God is reduced or eliminated. Through salvation, we have been made the righteousness of God. That means we have a right to stand before God as if we have never sinned. We can go boldly before the throne of grace to receive mercy and help in times of need. If we sin, we can be cleansed immediately, as we confess our sin with sincere regret. Without this consciousness, we rob ourselves of fellowship with the Father. We bear needless pains and burdens, because we misunderstand our relationship with God.

Our salvation has provided physical and material prosperity. We do not need to be sick or poor. Without this enlightenment, we will accept sickness and lack, which make us unable to fulfill the plan of God for our lives in the best way possible. Our bodies are temples of the Holy Spirit, and he needs us healthy, so we can be used by God more effectively. It costs money to accomplish the things we are assigned to do. If we do not understand that God supplies our needs, we will accept lack and not progress as we should.

Our salvation has provided emotional health. Jesus gave us His peace. Without this knowledge, we will accept confusion and depression. Like many around us, we will say things like, "This is driving me crazy." The peace of God enables us to stay calm, when it would otherwise be impossible. When we stay calm, we remain under control. When we are under control, we can make better decisions. When we make better decisions, we become more of an asset to the Kingdom of God.

Let us study all that is included in our salvation, and put our helmets on snugly. God wants us to be effective, and we owe it to Him to give our best.

I will be aware of my salvation and what is included in it. I will be an asset to the Kingdom of God.

Day 98

Hebrews 11:27

"By faith he forsook Egypt, not fearing the wrath of the king: for he endured, as seeing Him who is invisible."

Moses was able to deal with Pharaoh fearlessly. He left Egypt with sufficient courage to make it all the way to the promised land. The only reason he could endure the things he faced, from the beginning to the end, was he was able to see something beyond the natural realm.

The author of Hebrews said Moses saw Him who was invisible. When there is no natural reason to go on, only the assurance that we have supernatural help enables us to press forward. Endurance is produced by focusing on a goal, believing we can make it all the way.

We must first, however, have a goal - a purpose. As Christians, the most important goal for us is completing our divine assignment. We should want our lives to count. The love of God in us should make us reach out with a desire to help as many people as we can.

Secondly, we must know we have the strength to make it. Paul once thought God had to deliver him from the assignment Satan had brought against him. He was bothered over and over again, no matter where he went. After a while, he felt as though he could not take any more. Then, the Lord informed him of the power of grace that was his. His concern was over. He happily moved forward, realizing he had what he needed to win and defeat every attack of the devil. He acknowledged that when he had run out of his own ability, the power of Christ would rest upon him. Not only was that comforting to Paul, but it was thrilling. He boasted about his own inability, so he could experience the power of Christ upon him.

Let us focus on Jesus, the author and finisher of our faith. Let us follow His example. He concentrated on the reward before Him, to produce the endurance he needed to reach the end of the race.

I will focus on the Lord, who is the source of my strength. I will endure to the end, knowing that a reward awaits me, if I go all the way.

Day 99
Malachi 3:6 NIV

"I the Lord do not change. So you, O descendants of Jacob, are not destroyed."

God's patience is remarkable. His endurance and mercy are beyond description. He keeps His Word, even when we fail to do our part. In Malachi 3:6, it looked like God had run out of every reason, except for His integrity, to refrain from destroying Israel. Yet, He still loved them.

The goodness of God should lead us to repentance. When we consider how merciful He has been to us, despite our unfaithfulness, we should fall down and worship Him. There is none like our Father. He is rich in mercy and loving kindness, and His love for us cannot be matched. What we see in God should make us do all we can to serve Him faithfully and bless Him continually.

Let us look at the Father today and be changed. Let us cancel our plans to do wrong today, no matter what may tempt us. Whoever we may have planned to retaliate against, let us forgive, release and bless them in the name of the Lord. If we would give away all the mercy we receive, we would never punish anyone ever again.

I will examine myself today. If I need to repent for past sins or unfaithfulness, I will. If I need to repent for things I am tempted to do today, with God's help I will. I will live this day, mindful of the mercy of God toward me, so I can show more love toward my fellow man.

Day 100
Romans 8:1

"There is therefore now no condemnation to them which are in Christ Jesus, who walk not after the flesh, but after the Spirit."

In Romans Chapter 7, Paul described the spiritual warfare he experienced. He would do wrong when he really wanted to do right. In verse 24, he asked who could deliver him from his wretched condition. Then, in the next verse, he declared that victory comes through Jesus Christ. This preface must be read to understand Romans 8:1.

The "therefore" in Romans 8:1 is there, because of Romans 7:25. There is no condemnation to those in Christ Jesus, because Christ gives us the victory in the war against sin. Romans 8:2 says the law of the Spirit of life, under which we now operate, has freed us from the law of sin and death. We are never unable to resist sin. Sin is what produces death.

Paul encouraged the Roman Christians to see themselves as those who walk after the spirit and not the flesh. We have complete victory over sin, but we must still exercise our wills-- our choices to walk in what is ours.

There is no condemnation to us who are in Christ. There is no need to beat ourselves over the head for sins and failures, as though we are helpless. If we fall, we must face the fact that we do so, because we choose to walk after the flesh - not because we could not help it. So, we should just repent and get back to walking in the spirit. That does not mean we should take sin lightly. We should be truly sorry and have honest repentance. However, it does not profit us to permit condemnation, since that would be participating with Satan, instead of God.

God does not wink at sin, but he does not want us to magnify failure. When we are sincere, He is ready to forgive, cleanse and lift us. Our Father wants to restore us and take us higher in Him, where we fail less and less, and please Him more and more. Our enemy, Satan, on the other hand, wants to condemn us and discourage us, so we will feel unworthy to serve God. He would like to discourage us until we fall lower and lower and please God less and less.

Let us open our eyes, then, and see the forces on both sides. Let us choose God's side. As long as our Lord reaches out to us, let us disappoint the devil and respond pleasingly to Our Father, who loved us so much that He sent Jesus to die in our stead.

I will turn away from the road to condemnation and follow the road to restoration. With God's help, I will live higher above sin every day.

Day 101
Psalm 21:7

"For the king trusteth in the Lord, and through the mercy of the Most High he shall not be moved."

David went through many challenges in his life. He had some tremendous victories. He also made some very foolish and costly mistakes. David's failures were enough to cause anyone to become completely discouraged with himself and doubtful about having a healthy relationship with God again. However, David believed in God's mercy. After honest repentance, he received that mercy and lived to be an old man--his relationship with God still intact.

Most of us have not messed up "big time" as David did, measuring by human standards. Yet, in whatever ways we have fallen short, we are often tempted to feel permanently defeated. We will probably continue being Christians, but our zeal and excitement may have diminished in some aspects of our lives. Subconsciously, we may begin to relate to circumstances based on our shortcomings. Now, some things are obvious connections to our past. However, unless the Holy Spirit shows us this connection, it is not our business to guess or assume. On the other hand, if He <u>does</u> show us, then, God's grace will help us through these things and make it easier for us.

    Let us remember that we cannot punish ourselves without insulting the blood of Jesus. Even in the things we suffer for obvious reasons, we are to respect the blood and expect God's grace to create good from our negative circumstances. We must always, like David, trust in the Lord and rely on His mercy. It is a gift, not an earned reward. Then, we too, will not be moved. May we be inspired to go full steam ahead, having put away every self-created weight, as we endeavor to avoid vain imaginations that rob God of the pleasure of making us all we can be.

I will trust in and rely confidently on the Lord, knowing that through His mercy and steadfast love, I will remain firmly planted in Him. I will forget the past and let every day be a new day of adventure with Him, not assuming anything is a hindrance, unless He has revealed such to me. Even with obvious hindrances created by my own doings, I will expect His grace to assist me. Regardless of the mistakes of the past or shortcomings of the present, I will rely on God's love for me and His divine ability to make me all I can be. I am going for the gold!

Day 102
I Peter 2:24

"Who His own self bare our sins in His own body on the tree, that we, being dead to sins, should live unto righteousness: by whose stripes ye were healed."

Should we feel trapped by sin, as though we are powerless against it? What an insult it would be to the sacrifice Jesus made for us, for a child of God to accept defeat by sin. Jesus bore our sins in His body at Calvary, so we could be liberated from the power of darkness. We are also delivered from sickness and disease, because He took all of it upon Himself. Because of the stripes he bore, we are delivered from sin and sickness.

We must declare our victory over all the works of darkness. The songwriter wrote that we are signifying the Lord's death until He comes. When we do this, we should be reminding ourselves of what He took for us, so we can be free.

I declare victory over sin, sickness and disease. Because of what Jesus did for me, I am free.

Day 103
James 5:14

"Is any sick among you? Let him call for the elders of the church; and let them pray over him, anointing him with oil in the name of the Lord:"

It is interesting to note that James asked, "Is there any sick among you?" It sounds like sickness among the Body of

Christ was not acceptable to them. James gave instructions to the church on how to get the sick back to health.

The leaders of the church in its early stages were intolerant of sickness and disease. There is no record of anyone giving God glory by remaining sick. James 5:15 said the elders' prayer of faith would save the sick, and the Lord would restore him. Although doctors and medicine were available during that time, that was not where the Christians were told to look for their deliverance. No one condemned the medical profession or gave any commands to shun physicians. Christians simply assumed that God was the source of their help. They also assumed that healing would always be the result.

James was very bold in his statement in verse 15 about the Lord raising up the sick. He used no "ifs" or "buts." Very matter-of-factly, he said God would raise them up. What is our attitude about sickness and disease? Do we tolerate it as just a normal part of life? Is seeking God's help a last resort?

Let us catch the spirit of James, relative to healing. If disease attacks our bodies, let us treat the occurrence as an illegal invasion. We must not flow with it, but resist it. If we need assistance, let us call for spiritual help first. May we look to God always and expect total victory, whether we use a doctor's help or not.

I will be intolerant of sickness and disease. If it comes my way, I will look to God as the source of my healing and health.

Day 104

Ezra 8:21 Amplified Version

"Then I proclaimed a fast there, at the river Ahava, that we might humble ourselves before our God, to seek from

Him a straight and right way for us, our little ones, and all our possessions."

King Cyrus of Persia had received a command from God to build the temple at Jerusalem. Once construction got underway, enemies began to interfere. Ezra, an Israelite priest, was coordinating the efforts to complete the project. There was danger along the route they had to travel, but Ezra was ashamed to request protection from the king. He had bragged to the king about God giving favor to all who seek Him.

Before they left for Jerusalem to take items they needed to complete the temple, Ezra proclaimed a fast. They were seeking God's direction.

Fasting allows us to quiet our bodies and tune in to the Spirit of God. To get the full benefit, we must not only abstain from food, but we must also seek God during the time we would normally be eating. It is important for us to realize that our helter-skelter behavior in times of crisis is not due to God hiding direction from us. We race about, because we do not take time to receive His guidance. Sometimes, receiving the insight we need requires more than just a few minutes of prayer and quietness before God. Fasting and dedicating our meal time to seeking God can make a tremendous difference in our ability to receive from Him. Jesus once told His disciples fasting could eliminate unbelief that would hinder mighty works of God from being performed through them.

We should be ashamed to fall desperately before the ungodly for help, when we have boasted about how great our God is. Surely, all we have said about God is true. So, let us seek His face for guidance as to how He plans for us to accomplish the tasks He has set before us. God is not haphazard. If He orders an ark to be built, the package always comes with specific instructions.

I will seek God for direction to accomplish the tasks set before me. When necessary, I will fast and pray, and God will give me revelation.

Day 105
Acts 13:2 Amplified Version

"While they were worshipping the Lord and fasting, the Holy Spirit said, Separate now for me Barnabas and Saul for the work to which I have called them."

While prophets and teachers were fasting and worshipping God in Antioch, they heard from God. The Holy Spirit revealed to them God's wisdom about a certain part of the apostolic ministry. Paul and Barnabas, who subsequently went on a successful missionary journey, were set apart for team ministry at that time.

It seems absurd to think of putting a bank card in a cash machine and going through the proper procedures, but not knowing cash is coming out. Although the money would come out in that instance, we could leave the machine empty handed. It is important that we know what to expect when we practice the Word of God. We can obtain this knowledge by reading in the Bible about those who served God.

In Acts 13, we see that the results of fasting and ministering to the Lord produced wisdom and direction. When we set aside time to fast and minister to the Lord, we should not walk away without looking for results. Sometimes, our failure to receive may not have been a lack of response on God's part. It could have been our lack of expectancy. We may have walked away after doing our part, instead of looking and waiting for God's response.

I will expect and wait for God's response to my ministry to Him. He always responds. I must always anticipate His response.

Day 106

Acts 13:3 Amplified Version

"Then after fasting and praying, they put their hands on them and sent them away."

Sometimes, a mission we are about to embark on can stretch our faith beyond the limits we have already experienced. According to Acts 13, the ministers who heard from God about Paul and Barnabas' ministry saw fit to fast before they sent them away. The church was still fairly young, and the trail Paul and Barnabas would be blazing was new. As Jesus pointed out in Matthew 27, fasting sometimes helps rid us of unbelief. As a result, our faith is strengthened.

Paul was about to face hostile Jews, who were rebellious against the message that Jesus was the Messiah. He would meet Gentiles, who were profiting from the worship of idol gods and would not sit quietly while their customers turned to the true God. Then, there were the intellectuals, who would scoff at the idea of someone being raised from the dead. Most of all, there was the unknown, which could always have brought fear.

Denying the flesh and concentrating on spiritual things through fasting and prayer always strengthens the spirit and allows faith to increase. Paul and Barnabas, along with the other ministers at Antioch, were very wise to fast and pray before launching their challenging ministry. May we humbly see and follow their example, as we are lead by the Spirit of God. We must know, however, that we are fasting to prepare ourselves and not to guarantee successful ministry. Successful ministry is guaranteed by obedience to God and by faith.

I will fast and pray to prepare myself for ministry. I will fast and pray to get rid of unbelief and to strengthen my faith.

Day 107
Genesis 1:1

"In the beginning God created the heaven and the earth."

It is of no small significance that the Bible tells us of the preeminence of God. If anything began before Him, then our search would not begin or end with Him. However, knowing that nothing came into existence without Him enables us to recognize where our total source is. For some reason, we often seem to forget this simple fact. Perhaps, we forget to acknowledge His proper position because we do not see Him with our physical eyes. That is why the Bible teaches us to walk by faith and not by sight.

Genesis 1:1 is not regarded as a particularly outstanding scripture that affects our daily living. However, when we grasp the impact of this verse, we may reconsider how often we should meditate on it. If we owned a product and needed help understanding how it worked, we might ask someone we thought was knowledgeable about it. If, while consulting that person, the maker of the product walked in, the attention of everyone would probably go immediately to him. Who would know better how something operates than the one who made it?

If we were attempting to get more understanding about an incident to help us know how to respond properly, we would look for people who were there when it happened. It would probably help us if someone, who had insight into why it happened, could be found.

How much more would we seek God for help, if we were aware that He were the creator of everything, and that He was here before anything existed? He has insight into the reason for every incident that occurs on earth.

We forget sometimes that God has the answer to everything. Sometimes, we simply forget He is present. Let us celebrate both His preeminence and His presence today. It will help life go easier. We will turn to Him first and not as a last resort, when we finally remember who He is and where He is.

I will celebrate the preeminence of God and His presence. As a result, I will more easily overcome life's challenges.

Day 108
Jeremiah 23:16

"Thus saith the Lord of hosts, Hearken not unto the words of the prophets that prophesy unto you: they make you vain: they speak a vision of their own heart, and not out of the mouth of the Lord."

Jeremiah proclaimed to the nation of Israel that the prophets they were listening to had not heard from God. He said they were false prophets, declaring their own visions. They had not spent time with God. From their own minds came visions that would tickle the ears of listeners.

An important observation here is that the prophets had not spent time with God. All of us have creative minds given us by our Creator. Whether men are saved or lost, their minds affect the quality of life they will enjoy, as their ideas are transformed into goods and services. Since we all have the ability to get visions from our imaginations, as Christians we must spend time with God to be certain our visions do not conflict with His. (The word "vision" refers to our goals and plans, not just dreams or apparitions.)

Our own dreams and plans may be exciting and motivating. However, spending time with God can save us time and money. It can spare us disappointment and frustration. It is good for us to see clearly from the natural perspective, but as people of God, we have an advantage we should use. We can see from God's perspective and adjust our plans accordingly. A songwriter wrote that we forfeit peace, and bear needless pains when we do not carry everything to God in prayer. If we do not take advantage of the counsel available to us, we deserve all the trouble we encounter.

Let us submit our plans for approval. Perhaps the plans were put in our hearts by God. That does not excuse us from checking with Him on our strategy. Our walk with God should be one of consistent fellowship. His complete plans for our lives are often revealed line upon line, precept upon precept, here a little, there a little.

I will stay in constant fellowship with God. He will give me visions for my life and ministry. I will receive both the vision and the strategy to flow with it step by step.

Day 109
I Corinthians 15:57

"But thanks be to God, which giveth us the victory through our Lord Jesus Christ."

God gives us victory, so we should not feel we must earn it. We were unable to obtain it for ourselves. Our heavenly Father sent His only begotten Son to suffer and die, descend into Hell, and be raised from the dead for us.

Colossians 2:14 tells us the evidence of our guilt and unworthiness was nailed to the cross, where Jesus died. That freed us from doom. The forces of darkness would have kept us bound, but verse 15 reveals that Jesus triumphed over them. God did not need to fight them for His sake. Darkness was never a threat to Him. It was done for us. Jesus became a man and represented us in the battle of the ages. He won! Therefore, we win!

Let us lift our hearts, our heads and our voices today and declare our victory boldly and proudly. We cannot brag on ourselves, but we are certainly proud of our Savior. What a privilege to be children of the Most High God. May we accept our victory with an attitude of gratitude. First, we must act as though we believe God. Then, we must let our dedication to Him demonstrate appreciation.

I believe God has given me victory. I will conduct myself accordingly. I will demonstrate my appreciation through my dedication to Him.

Day 110
Psalm 27:1

"The Lord is my light and my salvation; whom shall I fear? the Lord is the strength of my life; of whom shall I be afraid?"

Since God is our Creator, it is obvious that we owe all honor and praise to Him for all we are able to do naturally. When the psalmist, David, said the Lord was his light and salvation and the strength of his life, he was recognizing God as his source for more than just natural things. He was declaring his acceptance of God as a personal Savior. That enabled David to receive supernatural help. He experienced strength he would not have had within the boundaries of human limitations.

A songwriter wrote that the blood (referring to the blood of Jesus) that gives strength on a daily basis would never lose its power. He was alluding to a source of strength that surpasses human ability.

Jesus referred to Himself as a vine, and to us as branches that draw life from the vine. He cautioned us that we must stay connected to Him to avoid becoming useless. There is a supernatural source of power available to us, but only if we choose to benefit from it.

Let us choose to draw strength from God today. Like David, may we, from our hearts, declare the Lord to be the strength of our lives. As we declare it, let us realize that we need to stay connected to Him to be able to go beyond our natural abilities. He will help us do what we cannot do without Him, and we will glorify Him for it.

The Lord is the strength of my life. I remain connected to Him, thereby drawing life from Him. I will glorify Him for all I can do, because of His life flowing in and through me.

Day 111
Deuteronomy 7:2

"And when the Lord thy God shall deliver them before thee; thou shalt smite them, and utterly destroy them; thou shalt make no covenant with them, nor shew mercy unto them:"

In the Old Testament times, the enemies of the Israelites were people who served idol gods. When they arrived at the promised land, the people of God were assigned to destroy the heathen there, who would seek to turn them away from the true

God. They were not permitted to make deals with them, or show mercy to them.

Today, under the New Covenant, we are not fighting flesh and blood, but our attitude against our spiritual enemies should be the same. We have been given the privilege of occupying a spiritual promised land. To do so, we must annihilate the enemies that would hinder us from entering in and taking full possession of what Jesus paid for us to have. God said He has provided us with health, peace, prosperity and victory over sin. Jesus came that we might have abundant life. He was bruised for our transgressions and sicknesses, and he paid the price for our peace.

As we possess our promised land, let us not make deals with the enemy or show mercy towards him. May we press on, accepting nothing short of what has been guaranteed us. At times, it may have been tempting for the Israelites to make deals with their enemies, rather than to fight. However, God warned them that it would hurt them to do other than what they were told.

An examination of the church's attitude toward sickness will serve as an example of how our attitude towards our enemies will make a difference in the quality of our lives. When we look at the record of the New Testament church in its early stages, we see an intolerance for sickness. The apostle James told the church to call upon the elders if there were any sick among them. Over the years, sickness began to be tolerated among believers. It was no longer treated as an enemy. In some cases, it was even proclaimed to be a gift from God. (What an insult!) Now, we suffer with widespread doubt and unbelief in the church. Many are ill and unable to give what God has designed for them to contribute. Elders in James' day were told to pray the prayer of faith that would cause a healing to come to the sick. Today, elders pray the prayer of doubt that helps many sick get worse, or even die. Satan has kept health and life from many people, because they have made deals with him or shown mercy on their spiritual enemies.

Let God arise and His enemies be scattered! He will arise and perform on our behalf, when we arise and determine not to tolerate the enemy any longer.

I will examine my attitude toward the enemies I encounter in my life, as well as in the lives of others. I declare stepped up warfare against the enemies in my promised land. I have no mercy for my spiritual enemies, and I am not interested in making any deals with them.

Day 112
Acts 14:9-10

"The same heard Paul speak: who steadfastly beholding him, and perceiving that he had faith to be healed, Said with a loud voice, Stand upright on thy feet. And he leaped and walked."

Acts 14 records the marvelous healing of a man who was born a cripple and had never walked. He heard Paul preach the gospel and developed faith to be healed.

It is interesting to note that details about the content of Paul's message were not given. It was simply stated that he preached the gospel. This indicates that healing for the physical body through Christ is a very fundamental part of the gospel.

Over the years, in many circles, the gospel has been diluted. Doubt and unbelief have caused some to eliminate physical healing as part of the gospel. This account of Paul preaching at Lystra indicates that the first century Christians saw healing as a fundamental part of the good news about Jesus. Faith comes by hearing the Word of God. The crippled man could not get faith for healing, unless he heard it offered in a convincing manner. Paul convinced him by explaining the benefits of Jesus' mission to earth.

We must become convinced that healing is available to us through Jesus Christ. As we read the gospels, the book of Acts, and the letters to the churches, we should get a clear message that healing has been provided for us. The only thing that can hinder us and make the good news ineffective is our entertaining traditions that are contrary to the Bible. Jesus said to the religious leaders of His day in Matthew 15:6 (Amplified Version), "So for the sake of your tradition (the rules handed down by your forefathers), you have set aside the Word of God -- depriving it of force and authority and making it of no effect."

May we discard every tradition or any other hindrances to our receiving the benefit Jesus suffered to provide for us. He was brutally whipped 39 times, and the Word says with those stripes we were healed. Let us gratefully receive deliverance from sickness and disease.

I will build faith for healing, because it has been given to me. By the stripes of Jesus, I was healed.

Day 113
I Thessalonians 1:3 Amplified Version

"We ought and indeed are obligated [as those in debt] to give thanks always to God for you, brethren, as it is fitting, because your faith is growing exceedingly, and the love of every one of you each toward the others is increasing and abounds."

The God kind of faith is not of this world. Therefore, it is neither obtained or maintained by simple existence on this planet. Faith comes by hearing God's Word. Doing the Word, or acting on faith that comes keeps it alive. Faith that is not acted upon dies. As James said, "Faith without works is dead." If there is no corresponding action to our faith, it becomes useless.

Paul wrote to the Thessalonian Christians, expressing his gratitude to God for what he saw happening among them. One thing he observed was that their faith was growing. One way to maintain faith is to see that it grows. For faith to grow, it must continue to be fed faith food -- God's Word. Then it must be exercised. We must be doers. Also, since faith works by love, we must nurture our love walk by confessing and practicing love. Paul not only observed that the Thessalonians' faith was growing, but he also noticed an increase in the love they had toward each other.

Let us feed and exercise our faith today. Since we have a spiritual life to maintain, we need spiritual food and exercise, just like our physical bodies need physical food and exercise. Let us also nourish our love walk, which helps everything else function properly.

I will feed and exercise my faith today. I will also nurture my love walk. As a result, my faith will grow and be maintained.

Day 114

Psalm 29:11 Amplified Version

"The Lord will give [unyielding and impenetrable] strength to His people; the lord will bless His people with peace."

It is so comforting to know that as God's people, we have a source of supply that is not available to the world. How often have we wondered how we would make it with our natural strength? Then, when the strength of God kicked in, we were able to testify that because of Him, our mission was accomplished, and we were still standing.

The psalmist, David, said the Lord <u>will</u> give strength. He must have realized that every time he ran out of his own abilities, God's supernatural power came to keep him winning.

Our loving Father cares for us and is very particular about us. He always supplies what we need. Let us open up and receive from Him. Although we must do our part to take care of ourselves, He is a very present help when we need more than what we have to make it.

I am grateful for the divine supply that meets my human deficiency. I receive strength from God today to accomplish what needs to be done.

Day 115
Psalm 1:3

"And he shall be like a tree planted by the rivers of water, that bringeth forth his fruit in his season; his leaf also shall not wither; and whatsoever he doeth shall prosper."

In this verse, the psalmist describes the forecast of a person who meets the following criteria:

1. He does not follow ungodly counsel.
2. He does not stand in the path where sinners walk.
3. He does not participate in scorning or mocking.
4. His delight is in the law of God.
5. He habitually mediates God's Word day and night.

This person will experience victory at all times. Like a tree planted by the river, he will never be away from his source of life. Consequently, his due season will always be on time. He will never dry up, and all he does will prosper.

It is easy to understand how that kind of godly living will produce prosperity. Romans 8:6 says, "...to be spiritually minded is life and peace." When we give God's Word priority in our lives and separate ourselves from all that displeases the Lord, we cannot help but win. That does not mean we will not face challenges or obstacles. It means we will always win in the end.

When we really understand what God's commands are for, we can easily delight in them. They are not just to restrict us, but rather to benefit us. I John 5:3 tells us they are not grievous or burdensome. So, let us pray today that our spiritual eyes will be opened to understand the sweetness of God's Word, so we will have no difficulty in habitually mediating it.

I will follow only godly advice and stay in the paths of righteousness. I will refrain from scorning or mocking. I will absolutely delight in God's Word and habitually meditate it. Everything I do will prosper.

Day 116
I Corinthians 9:27 Amplified Version

"But [like a boxer] I buffet my body -- handle it roughly, discipline it by hardships --- and subdue it, for fear that after proclaiming to others the Gospel and things pertaining to it, I myself should become unfit -- not stand the test and be unappproved -- and rejected [as a counterfeit]."

Our bodies will not experience full redemption until Jesus calls us to Heaven. When, in the twinkling of an eye, we exchange corruption for incorruption and mortality for immortality, we will collect the balance of what is due us in the redemption of our bodies. Meanwhile, our bodies remain earthly. We are responsible for managing them properly.

As long as our bodies are in this world, we are subject to sickness and disease. To live in health, we must follow natural laws and take advantage of the spiritual laws given us, to make up for what natural laws cannot do.

Another part of being in the world is being subject to the lust of the flesh. Our bodies have feelings, and those feelings can lead us into temptation. Therefore, we must discipline ourselves to endure temptation and live above sin. Paul talked about disciplining and subduing his body, so he would not become unfit himself, after helping others to overcome. We must do the same, if we want to guarantee success. It is very important that we have a habit of roughing up our bodies and making them subject to our spirits.

Through fasting, we can teach our bodies that our bellies are not our gods. The lust for food has hindered people from obeying God. Like Jesus, we need to be able to miss a meal and say, "My meat is to do the will of Him that sent me."

Through exercise, which helps us maintain good health, we can teach our bodies to follow our commands. As our bodies learn to follow instructions, we will be able to obey the Holy Spirit and get up when we feel like sleeping. Our bodies will understand that they may not participate in sin, no matter how appealing it may be.

By strengthening our spirits, we stand a better chance of remaining healthy physically. We are also more likely to stay out of trouble. Our goal should always be to nourish our spirits more than our bodies. Spiritual domination will help eliminate fleshly failures. So, let us send a clear message today. May our bodies hear us say, "You will not eat more than you should. You will eat what I permit you to. You will exercise until I say it is enough. You will read, meditate and pray at my command and not at your convenience. You will obey me." ("I" and "me" represent the spirit inside, which God intends to dominate us, as He leads.)

I will discipline my body to assist my spirit. My body will not dominate me. I will fast, pray, and exercise, and do whatever the Holy Spirit leads, to establish the proper order of command: spirit, soul, then body.

Day 117
James 1:5 Amplified Version

"If any of you is deficient in wisdom, let him ask of the giving God [Who gives] to everyone liberally and ungrudgingly, without reproaching or faultfinding, and it will be given him."

Why would James suggest that we ask God for wisdom if we lacked it? It appears as though we should not accept a lack of wisdom in the time of need. James went on to say that God gives it liberally, without finding fault with us. That is indicative of God's desire for us to always have the understanding we need, as well as direction on how to proceed.

The Bible states in James 1:6 that we should ask in faith, without doubting, if we hope to receive wisdom from God. If we are told to have faith and not doubt, then that alone indicates that the wisdom is certainly available to us. If we know that it is available to us, then there is no need for doubt.

Since God gives wisdom generously, it is up to us how much we have. The limitations are not on His end. Proverbs contains several admonitions for us to get wisdom. Again, this shows that wisdom is available. Let us increase in wisdom today by asking for it and by confessing that we have it by faith. Solomon suggested that we call wisdom our sister and understanding our close friend.

I believe I receive wisdom from God today. Wisdom is

my sister and understanding, my close friend.

Day 118

II Corinthians 12:9

"And he said unto me, My grace is sufficient for thee: for my strength is made perfect in weakness. Most gladly therefore will I rather glory in my infirmities, that the power of Christ may rest upon me."

Most Christians have not suffered like the apostle Paul. Shipwrecks, stoning, imprisonment, constant harassment and rejection of his kinsmen did not stop him from fulfilling his calling. However, like a normal human, he became weary of the persecution the devil was sending his way time and time again. After seeking God about the matter three times, he received a revelation that would be the boost he needed to survive the long haul.

Jesus told Paul His grace was enough to put him over. Grace is God's ability given to us freely, although we can in no way deserve it. Paul learned that He had God's ability to overcome every test and trial. He also learned that he could discourage the devil by making him sorry for attacking him. As a result, the attacks eventually slacked off. In the latter years of Paul's life, he was free to preach and teach from a private house under government protection, free of harassment.

Paul said he would no longer be disgusted over inability. Jesus had revealed to him that in the moments of human weakness, divine strength becomes available and functions at its best. So, he became excited over the fact that the best time to enjoy the power of Christ taking over for him was when he was in his weakest moment.

As long as we can handle our affairs in our own strength, it is easy to forget that we have strength beyond our human limits. It is when we run out, that we are forced to seek that which is not inherently ours. It is then that we experience the wonderful power of God in manifestation. After experiencing this over and over, we will stop dreading weak moments. Weak moments are opportunities to experience God's power.

Whenever we are weak today, God's grace is sufficient for us. Christ's strength will be perfected in our weakness.

God will give me strength today to overcome all weakness. I have His grace. I have His strength. I am strong in God today.

Day 119
Psalm 32:8

"I will instruct thee and teach thee in the way which thou shalt go: I will guide thee with mine eye."

God has promised us instructions and teaching while we are on our journey in this life. We must expect to receive through the different methods He has given us. Jesus once said "He who has ears to hear, let him hear." If we are not expecting something, we can easily miss it. We can hear sounds and words, but miss what God is saying, because we are not anticipating his guidance.

In Psalm 32:8, the Lord said He would guide us with His eye. A stationary object cannot be guided. If we do not get in motion, we cannot be led. Sometimes, we will never know if we have chosen the right direction until we leave the place we are currently in. While we are progressing, we will sense the eye of the Lord approving or disapproving of our movement.

We must not be afraid to make a move. God is very liberal with wisdom and guidance. It is for His own name's sake that He freely gives instruction. We can only become proficient in following the Lord by stepping out and learning His voice, and His methods of divine guidance. He will always guide us perfectly, but we must learn how to flow perfectly with Him. The top of the ladder is reached one step at a time. Let us begin, or continue climbing today. We will, as we pray and fellowship with the Father, Son, and Holy Spirit.

I will listen for and receive teaching, instruction and guidance from God today. He will lead me, and I will follow.

Day 120
Job 36:5

"Behold God is mighty, and despiseth not any: he is mighty in strength and wisdom."

When we need wisdom, which is all the time, we need God. As Elihu said in Job 36:5, He is mighty in wisdom.

Jesus likened our relationship with Him to a vine and its branches. Branches cannot be fruitful when they are separated, because they draw their life from the vine. Even so, we must not expect to operate in wisdom, unless we are drawing it from the source of wisdom. We must do the things that cause us to suck life, power and wisdom from God. Prayer, praise and worship enable us to draw life from God. Communion, fellowship and quiet meditation also help. Reading and studying His Word make a difference. Praying in the Holy Spirit will also contribute to our success.

We always need wisdom, although sometimes it seems we need it more urgently than other times. Let us establish a constant flow between us and God. Today, may we increase what we are already doing to cause a greater flow of wisdom into our spirits.

I will increase in prayer, praise and worship. I will do more reading, studying and meditating of God's Word. More and more of His wisdom will flow into me, and I will walk in it.

Day 121
Psalm 51:6

"Behold, you desire truth in the inner being; make me therefore to know wisdom in my inmost heart."

The Bible tells us that God guides us by our spirits -- our innermost being. The spirit is also called the heart. Our spirits should rule over our minds and bodies, as we are led by the Holy Spirit. David recognized the importance of this spiritual order and asked in Psalm 51 to know wisdom in his heart.

The most important part of our being is our spirit. It is the part of us that is born again. Our bodies are temporary, but our spirits are eternal. Our minds will always be with us, but they assist us in this natural world with natural things, and sometimes they conflict with spiritual matters. The spirit of man is the part of us that is the primary communicator with God, who is a Spirit.

To function on a level higher than the natural realm we live in, we need spiritual wisdom -- wisdom in our spirits. Natural wisdom that comes to our minds is very helpful in this earth realm, but we are not of this world. We need natural wisdom to function here, but spiritual wisdom is what we need to fulfill our God-given mission on this planet.

Wisdom will come to our inmost heart, as we fellowship with God through prayer and the study of His Word. It will come not by ritualistic prayer and study, but prayer and study in an atmosphere where we are conscious of His presence and see ourselves as "sitting at His feet." This is done by choice, not feeling, although we may feel something at times.

I will pray and study in the presence of God. I will sit at His feet and learn of Him. He will impart wisdom into my inmost heart.

Day 122
Genesis 4:10 Amplified Version

"And [the Lord] said, What have you done? The voice of your brother's blood is crying to me from the ground?"

God told Cain that Abel's blood was crying to Him from the ground. In Genesis 4:11, He told Cain a curse had come upon him, because of the blood he had shed. The earth that received his brother's blood would not produce for him, as it had before. (Cain was a farmer.) It is amazing how nature reacts to evil. It is no wonder we see natural disasters. Although people sometimes blame them on God, our planet is designed to revolt against wickedness. Disasters occur because of the presence of evil and not due to acts of God, except in rare cases of divine judgment.

It is clear that drought, floods, and other weather conditions that hinder the earth from producing its full strength for men occur as a result of innocent blood crying from the ground. That is why it is so important for Christians to inhabit the land. It is because of God's blessing, through those who will yield to Him, that the earth is not completely void of productivity. We are the salt of the earth.

Hebrews 12:24 says Jesus' blood speaks of better things than Abel's blood. The blood of Jesus cries out for mercy. Wherever it is received, mercy abounds. This can help us to understand the significance of Jesus' blood. If human blood can cause the earth to refuse to produce as it should, then it is clear that blood is more than just red cells and white cells. Blood speaks and makes demands. Therefore, the blood of Jesus Christ, the Son of God, speaks and demands. It demands mercy instead of vengeance. That is why the songwriter wrote, "And there may I, though vile as he, wash all my sins away," and "sinners plunged beneath that flood, lose all their guilty stains." Revelation 12:11 says, "And they overcame him by the blood of the Lamb..."

May we understand, and appreciate more, the blood Jesus shed for us. Whenever we partake of communion and drink the grape juice, symbolic of His blood, let us understand the power we are accepting. Hear the demands the blood made, and agree with it as you drink.

I will have greater and greater respect for the blood of Jesus, and the communion cup that represents that blood. I receive what Jesus' blood demands for me.

Day 123
Genesis 9:4 Amplified Version

"But you shall not eat flesh with the life of it, which is its blood."

After the flood, God blessed Noah when he left the ark and gave him permission to eat any animal or plant he desired. However, he forbade him to eat meat with blood in it. He told him the life of the flesh was the blood.

This can help us understand why Jesus said in John 6:54, "Whoso eateth My flesh, and drinketh My blood, hath eternal life; and I will raise him up at the last day." To eat His flesh and drink His blood was to partake of His life. Since He had eternal life in Him, we automatically have eternal life in us by receiving His blood.

There is no eternal life outside the blood sacrifice of Jesus Christ. We must receive His blood by faith, or be without life. That is why nobody else could have served as a mediator between God and man. No other man could be the way to God. Buddha, Muhammed, Confucius and all the others had human blood with natural life. Jesus, the Son of God, was the only living human who had blood containing eternal life - the life of God.

When we partake of communion, we celebrate the eternal life received by the blood of Christ. May we have a greater appreciation for the blood represented by the cup.

I have received the body and blood of Jesus, by faith. I have eternal life in me.

Day 124

Genesis 9:6 Amplified Version

"Whoso sheds man's blood, by man shall his blood be shed, for in the image of God He made man."

In Genesis 9:5 and 6, God reveals the value of human life and establishes the law of capital punishment. This was written many years before the Mosaic law was established. God did not give many rules to Noah. Therefore, what He gave him had to be very important.

The first command God gave Noah after the flood was to be fruitful and multiply and replenish the earth. The second command was to refrain from eating blood, and the third was to avenge the blood of every human being who was murdered.

God highly values the blood (the life) of every man. His desire is for every human being to know Him and to fellowship with Him. Originally, He made man in His image. He intended for us to look like Him and act like Him. Every normal father is pleased to hear someone say a child has to be his, because he looks just like him. Imagine, then, the pain a father feels when he views the lifeless body of one of his own. God grieves the death of every man, because we are all his creation.

The Heavenly Father gave the ultimate sacrifice to prove His love for every human being. He gave His only begotten Son – He gave Himself. Jesus died and shed the most valuable of all blood to save everyone who would receive Him. He died to save us from spiritual death. If we would meditate on this until it becomes a revelation in our hearts, we would not need anything else to elevate our godly self-esteem.

May we value ourselves, as well as every other human being on this planet, because of the value God has placed upon us. Let us be on God's side, as we work together for the lives (spiritual and physical) of all people.

I will consider all life valuable, including my own. I will participate in saving lives – spiritual and physical.

Day 125
Exodus 12:13

"And the blood shall be to you for a token upon the houses where ye are: and when I see the blood, I will pass over you, and the plague shall not be upon you to destroy you, when I smite the land of Egypt."

We know the blood represents life. God told the Israelites to put the blood of a lamb (a type of the blood of Jesus) on their door posts, so the death angel would not touch them. The blood would symbolize life to that house – a shadow of the results of Calvary. This is where Jesus would conquer death by his sacrifice; by the shedding of His blood.

This helps us understand what is meant by "pleading the blood." To plead the blood means to claim protection from harm by applying the blood of Jesus to our lives. Just as the Israelites placed their confidence in the blood for protection as destruction came their way, we should also trust God to protect us, because of the blood of Jesus. The blood of Christ represents our redemption, our covenant and our new eternal life.

Now the blood was provided for the Israelites, but they had to apply it. Whether or not we use the same terminology, such as "pleading the blood," in some way we must make the benefits of Calvary applicable to our individual lives and circumstances. Just because something has been provided does not mean we will benefit from it. We must apply it. How do we do that? By the words of our mouth. So, let us lift up our voices and agree with God that the blood of Jesus makes a difference in our lives today. We are protected, because of the blood.

I declare that the blood of Jesus makes a difference in my life today. I am protected from every plot of the destroyer.

Day 126
Exodus 24:8

"Moses took the blood, and sprinkled it on the people, and said, Behold the blood of the covenant, which the Lord hath made with you concerning all these words."

Moses read the words of the covenant God made with Israel. A covenant is an agreement between two parties. The people heard their part and God's part. They told Moses they would be obedient and do all God instructed them to do. That meant they were accepting the covenant. Moses then sprinkled the blood of the covenant on them, indicating that the agreement was then in force.

The covenant could not be established without blood. Once the blood was applied, the covenant was irreversible – it was sealed forever. If we grasp this concept, it will be easier for us to understand the integrity of God's Word. God finalized the words of the Old Covenant with blood, and He performed everything He promised. In the part of the world where these things took place, blood was the most powerful symbol in making a covenant. Since the Old Covenant was sealed with the blood of the animals and God did not alter one word, how much more secure is the New Covenant, which was sealed by the blood of Jesus Christ?

Jesus promised His disciples many things before His departure. He said He would not leave them comfortless, but would send the Holy Spirit. He assured them that He would return for them, and they would be where He was. They were promised supernatural power to carry on His work on earth. He made other promises. Before He departed, while having communion with them, He said the grape juice they drank represented His blood of the New Testament. That meant when His blood was shed to ratify the New Covenant, all he promised was secured.

It is up to us now to receive the covenant. Like the children of Israel, we receive that covenant by agreeing to our part. They said they would be obedient to all God's instructions. As we receive communion (an act of accepting the blood of the covenant), may we remember that it is a way of saying we will be obedient to all of God's Word. He is always faithful to keep His Word to us.

I will be obedient to all the instructions I receive from God. I will remember my part of the covenant, as well as God's part, when I partake of Holy Communion.

Day 127
Proverbs 4:18

"But the path of the just is as the shining light, that shineth more and more unto the perfect day."

It is thrilling to know that there is more of God to be revealed to us; more knowledge, more understanding and more wisdom. Whatever our current struggles may be, with Christ in us, we have the hope of overcoming every challenge. We will still win, despite the fact that we are still seeking wisdom in many areas, because our path is getting brighter all the time. Insight we do not have today will come tomorrow. We will continue to increase, until we arrive at perfection.

So, let us not give up, for giving up is the only way to lose. The psalmist said we should wait on the Lord and be of good courage, so He could strengthen our spirits. A strong spirit in a man will sustain him through difficult times.

Our path is getting brighter, not dimmer. May we remember that when circumstances declare something contrary to God's Word. We walk by faith. Paul said the spirit of faith declares what it believes. So, let us declare today, since we believe God's Word, that our path is shining more and more, as we head for perfection.

My path is getting brighter and brighter as I move toward perfection. Regardless of what it looks like now, my chances of winning are getting greater every moment.

Day 128
Malachi 4:2

"But unto you that fear my name shall the Sun of righteousness arise with healing in his wings; and ye shall go forth, and grow up as calves of the stall."

The prophet, Malachi, had a message for those who reverenced the name of the Lord. The Sun of Righteousness would arise with healing in His wings for them, and they would leap playfully, like calves released from the stall.

To reverently fear someone's name, one must have great respect for the person. A name only has worth, because of the quality of the person who bears that name. If we fear the name of the Lord, we fear the Lord Himself.

The more we respect someone, the more likely we are to cooperate with them. Our level of reverence for God is evident by our lifestyles. Jesus said our love for Him is demonstrated by our obedience to His commands.

Let us remind ourselves of two things. First, the commands of God are not to make life hard, but for our benefit and protection. Secondly, obedience to God produces great benefits. If we walk in line with God's will, we will not feel that we must earn healing, but we position ourselves for the Sun of Righteousness (Jesus Christ) to arise with healing, health, strength and joy <u>for</u> us.

I will always reverently fear the name of the Lord. My reverence will be shown by my obedience to Him. The Sun of Righteousness will arise with healing, health, strength, and joy for me.

Day 129
Malachi 4:2

"But unto you that fear my name shall the Sun of righteousness arise with healing in his wings; and ye shall go forth, and grow up as calves of the stall."

God always wants to be a blessing to all who will allow Him. Every organized system will produce what it was designed to produce, if the proper procedures are followed. God is totally organized. He has designed His system to produce blessings. James 1:17 said every good and perfect gift comes from God. We learn from Malachi 4:2 that healing is in God's system, and the procedure for obtaining it is having reverence for the name of the Lord. Healing has been provided for us through Jesus Christ, but everyone is not experiencing it.

When we respect someone's name, our behavior in regards to the person demonstrates that respect. If someone makes a request to us in the name of a particular dignitary, our response will be in accordance with the respect we have for that name, or that person. A name represents the person. How we respond to a name is not based on the sound of the letters used to spell it, but who is represented by that name.

Before we dogmatically declare that we reverence the name of the Lord, let us forget the religious acts we perform, and rather examine our reaction to God's messages sent to us. We receive requests in His name through the Bible, the Holy Spirit speaking to our spirits, the gifts of the Spirit, and perhaps a few other ways. In any case, it is important to remember that it is our response to God's direction and instructions for our lives that determine our level of reverence for His name. Our respect for the name of the Lord will cause us to have faith in whatever He says. Faith is what brings results.

Let us confess that we have respect for the name of the Lord and then act like it. Just as we train children to respect others, we can train ourselves to respect God's name. As we discipline ourselves to respect the name of the Lord, we can boldly say, "The Sun of righteousness will arise with healing in His wings for me."

I reverence the name of the Lord. His name is the highest name. There is no name above the name of the Lord. I will discipline myself to increase my level of respect for His name.

Day 130
Psalm 68:1

"Let God arise, let his enemies be scattered: let them also that hate him flee before him."

The psalmist, David, saw his enemies as God's enemies. He always depended on divine help in battle. His attitude was one of confidence in God and, since he and God were on the same side, the enemies did not stand a chance. Therefore, when he said, "Let God arise," he thought of himself going to battle with no chance of losing, because God was with him.

We, too, must see ourselves always winning because of who is on our side. In II Corinthians 2:14, Paul offered thanks to God who "always causes us to triumph in Christ Jesus." He also said in Romans 8:31, "If God be for us, who can be against us?" Then, in Romans 8:37, he said, "in all these things, we are more than conquerors through him that loved us."

Now, it is important that we realize that since God gave us the ability to choose in every area of life, we have to choose victory. When David said, "Let God arise," he saw himself going out to fight and Heaven backing him up. He did not see himself in bed complaining, while the angels did all the work. God arose when David arose. Even though it seemed at times that David did very little to accomplish his victories, he did initiate the fight. He did not expect divine action without his cooperation.

As we face opposing forces today, may we rise up on the inside. Let us see our battles as God's battles and say, "Let God arise, and His enemies be scattered." Then after saying that, let us do what we know to do, as we anticipate divine assistance to assure us victory.

I will arise today to meet every challenge with confidence. I will see God arising every time I arise. God will help me, and I will win every battle.

Day 131
Proverbs 21:30

"There is no wisdom nor understanding nor counsel against the Lord."

We know that wisdom is important and that following it will always bring the most desirable results. Therefore, the path of wisdom should always be followed. The main challenge before us is learning to discern what wisdom is speaking. Solomon gave us a clue in Proverbs 21:30. He said there is no wisdom that will counsel you against God.

Nobody's advice is better than the advice and counsel we get through the Word of God and by the Holy Spirit. In our day and time, we see more and more educated idiots. People who have graduated from universities are coming up with counsel that goes contrary to the Bible. They are even attempting to create laws that forbid us from obeying God's Word. It is insane to think that our society will prosper, when we attempt to outsmart our Creator. We have already suffered grave consequences for such ridiculous behavior.

Let us remember that one sure way to goof up is by choosing guidance that goes contrary to the Bible or the Holy Spirit's leading in our spirits. (The Holy Spirit will never lead us contrary to the written Word.) May we choose to always obey God, since anything else would be stupid.

I will follow wisdom by always walking in line with God's leading through the Bible and by the Holy Spirit guiding my spirit.

Day 132
Mark 4:39

"And he arose, and rebuked the wind, and said unto the sea, Peace, be still. And the wind ceased, and there was a great calm."

When Jesus left His peace with us, He was leaving us a great calm. He was leaving us the ability to cease from raging on the inside. We can be still.

In Mark 4:39, the word "peace" is followed by the words "be still." As we examine ourselves to see how we are maintaining our God-given peace, let us notice if we begin to get agitated. If necessary, we must speak to ourselves and command our souls and bodies to be still.

Since Jesus gave us peace, we do not need to ask for it. We must express thanks, as we acknowledge receiving it. Then, we must maintain it. We can have peace inside, in the midst of a storm outside, but we cannot have inner peace at the same time we are having an inner storm. Just as the winds and waves must be still to have peace in a physical storm, our inner turmoil must cease to have inner peace. We will calm our inner storms just as Jesus calmed the natural storm. With the peace He has given us, we can speak peace to our storms and command them to be still.

I receive and will maintain the peace Jesus left for me. I command every inner turmoil in me to be still. I am at peace.

Day 133
Exodus 13:3

"And Moses said unto the people, Remember this day, in which ye came out from Egypt, out of the house of bondage; for by strength of hand the Lord brought you out from this place: there shall no leavened bread be eaten."

It is interesting to note that Moses told Israel that the Lord brought them out of Egypt by "strength of hand." The expression, "strength of hand" denotes personal involvement, as well as strength.

When we say someone had a "hand" in doing something, we mean they were involved. If we say it was by the strength of their hand, we mean without their help, it could not have been done.

When we are being oppressed by the enemy, God is not pleased. If we sincerely look to Him as our source of help, He will arise and become personally involved in our deliverance. If we practice seeing God as our help, our confidence level will rise. The challenges of life will diminish in our eyes, as we realize the strength of His hand is on our side.

It is good to meditate on Exodus 13:3 and allow our minds to recapture the scenes that led to the deliverance of the Israelites from Egypt. It will give us an image of the power available to use through the hand of God. Isaiah 59:1 says,

"Behold the Lord's hand is not shortened, that it cannot save." In other words, the same strength demonstrated in the deliverance of Abraham's seed from Egypt is available to us now. God has not lost any strength, and all of it is available to deliver us and help us.

Let us lift up our heads and change our sad countenance to a joyful one if we need to. God is God. He is the only God. We have omnipotence on our side. We can be strong in the Lord and in the power of His might.

I will meditate on the strength of the Lord's hand. I will rejoice in the fact that His hand is available to me. I will use that knowledge to encourage myself.

Day 134
Psalm 16:8

"I have set the Lord always before me: because he is at my right hand, I shall not be moved."

There is a sure way for us to move with confidence. It is to know that the Lord is at our right hand, that He supports what we are doing. The psalmist said he set the Lord always before him. He did not allow the Lord to get out of his sight. To do that, he had to meditate God's Word continually, since he could not always physically see God. That caused him to make godly decisions. When he made godly decisions, he was confident that God was with him.

If we go our own way without consulting God or choose to go against the Bible, we cannot have full assurance of victory when we are challenged. It is best for us to do as Solomon said in Proverbs 3:5 and 6. He advised us to rely on God and not our own understanding, and to acknowledge Him so we can receive direction.

Let us pause and examine how much we keep the Lord before us. Have we gotten so busy doing things our own way, because we are very intelligent and know quite well how to run our affairs alone? Are we seeking God only when we have a need and do not know how to get it met? The Lord should be always before us. Sometimes, when we think we need Him the least is when we need Him most.

I will keep the Lord always before me. He will remain at my right hand and my confidence will be strong.

Day 135
Zechariah 12:10

"And I will pour upon the house of David, and upon the inhabitants of Jerusalem, the spirit of grace and supplications: and they shall look upon me whom they have pierced, and they shall mourn for him, as one mourneth for his only son, and shall be in bitterness for him, as one that is in bitterness for his firstborn."

Zechariah prophesied about Israel's future. In the twelfth verse, he said the day would come when the Jews would mourn for Jesus, whom they pierced. Hundreds of years would pass before He was pierced, and thousands of years before they would mourn for Him. Prophecy is a remarkable thing. This prophecy shows us that God is fully aware of the future.

If we know that it is going to rain today, we will plan accordingly. We would probably carry our umbrellas and raincoats with us. We would be sure our car windows are rolled up. We would probably plan indoor activities whenever possible. Our Father knows when it will rain or shine in our lives, and He has made preparations for us. Whenever we are taken by surprise, let us remember two things. First, God is not surprised, and He has a plan we can get in on, if we connect to Him. So, we can remain calm and in control. Secondly, may we be reminded that our walk with Him needs to get closer and closer, so we are not surprised as much.

Three Hebrew men were once placed in a fiery furnace (Daniel 3), but they were not afraid. They were confident that their future was secure, because they had committed it to God. God showed up because of their faith, but He did not come up with a plan on the spot. He knew long before then how He would deliver them.

Part of the ministry of the Holy Spirit is to show us things to come. As we fellowship with Him more, we will be taken by surprise less and less. Let us allow Him to increase our sense of security. Even when we do not know what the future holds, we can rest, knowing that He plans only good for our future.

I will fellowship more with the Holy Spirit. I will be surprised less and less. I will remain calm and in control, knowing that God has a good plan for me.

Day 136
Romans 4:16

"Therefore it is of faith that it might be by grace; to the end the promise might be sure to all the seed; not to that only which is of the law, but to that also which is of the faith of Abraham; who is the father of us all,"

Paul noted in Romans 4 that God's promise to Abraham was made to his seed through the righteousness of faith, so we could all benefit. In other words, since we are Abraham's seed by faith, we are included with the natural seed, when it comes to Abraham's blessing.

Romans 4:16 said the promise depends on faith, so it could be sure to us who are Abraham's seed by faith. When something is sure, it is guaranteed. There is no risk involved. A guaranteed promise gives us security. We do not need to wonder about whether or not we are entitled to it. No discussion is necessary. All we need to do is accept it.

I accept Abraham's blessings as mine. I am Abraham's seed by faith and, therefore, an heir of the promise to him.

Day 137
John 10:10

"The thief cometh not, but for to steal, and to kill, and to destroy: I am come that they might have life, and that they might have it more abundantly."

How do we feel about living today? Does it correspond to Jesus' intentions for us? If we are not enjoying an overflowing life, then we are disconnected, at least in part, from the plan of God through Jesus Christ. If He came to provide abundant living, He did not fail. There is no failure in Christ.

There are many facets to our abundant life. We can see them like the many gadgets in our houses that make them modern dwellings. There is an object we operate to cause running water to come out. There is another that causes lights to come on, and another that starts the central air climate control system. All these systems are connected to sources outside the home. If something does not work, we do not automatically assume the fault is with the source. We examine the machinery that makes the connection. Although natural sources can malfunction, nothing is ever wrong with our spiritual source. God does not fail. The fault is always in our connections. It is important that we know what to expect, so we can know when we need to check our connections. Jesus has provided a full, enjoyable life. Of course, that is not to be interpreted in worldly terms. The world cannot understand a man in a developed society who would happily give his life to minister to primitive people who have no modern conveniences. Enjoying a full life in Christ is an inner satisfaction and fulfillment. It is lacking nothing necessary to fulfill our divine purpose with joy.

As we examine our lives, if something is missing, we can check our manual, the Bible, and make sure our connections are right. One thing we must examine is our words. The Bible indicates that two people cannot walk together in disagreement. So, we must be sure we are saying what God says and not contradicting Him.

Another point of examination is our actions. Jesus said the doer of the Word is blessed. God told Joshua that as he did what he meditated on in the Word, he would be successful and prosperous.

We need to check our status today. If abundant life is not in any facet of our existence, then we must adjust our connections and let the life of Christ flow in.

I will have abundant life in every area of my existence. I will adjust all connections in every area where God's life is not evident. My life will be full.

Day 138

Proverbs 3:8

"It shall be health to thy navel, and marrow to thy bones."

The book of Proverbs contains wise sayings for many areas of life. One of the areas covered is physical health. Because we see this book as a spiritual book, we have not recognized the medical value in it. Many statements in this collection of wise sayings give us a connection between spiritual and physical well-being. Proverbs 3:8 reveals the natural, physical effect verses one through seven have on our body.

The verses preceding the eighth verse in the third chapter of Proverbs are not just for spiritual benefit. They literally affect our physical well-being. Verses one and two encourage us to be faithful to God's Word and receive long life as a result. We will live longer, with less stress, if we continually remember and keep the Word of God. The third and fourth verses tell us the results of operating in mercy and truth. If we live closely with mercy and truth, our lives would be less stressful, because we will be highly favored and esteemed by God and man.

Verses five and six advise us to put God first in our decision making. When we trust and are confident in God, leaning and relying fully on Him, instead of our own understanding, we will make better decisions. As we acknowledge Him in all our ways, He will direct our steps. Again, we will relieve ourselves of stress, which has a negative affect on our physical health.

The seventh verse tells us not to think we are smarter than we really are. It admonishes us to reverently fear and worship the Lord. If we follow that advice, we will stay away from evil and experience positive results in our entire body.

Let us realize that spiritual things affect our physical health. Let us use that knowledge to motivate us to be more diligent to live reverently in respect to God and His Word.

I will increase my reverence for God and His Word. I will be healthier.

Day 139
Daniel 4:36,37 NIV

"At the same time that my sanity was restored, my honor and splendor were returned to me for the glory of my kingdom. My advisors and nobles sought me out, and I was restored to my throne and became even greater than before. Now I, Nebuchadnezzar, praise and exalt and glorify the King of heaven, because everything he does is right and all his ways are just. And those who walk in pride he is able to humble."

In Daniel 4, the story of King Nebuchadnezzar's humiliation is a reminder to us that our high estate can be reduced to nothing in a moment, if we forget our source. The king was extremely proud of his accomplishments and boasted about them as though he, by his own might and intelligence, had brought about all his success. Daniel told him that for seven years, he would look and act like an animal, until he acknowledged that the Most High is sovereign over the kingdoms of men and gives them to anyone he wishes.

Such humiliation was not necessary, except that it was the only way Nebuchadnezzar would recognize that he was nothing without God. He had to realize that God allowed his success and could end it at anytime. What a pity it would be if we had to endure extreme humiliation as Christians because of not realizing who we are and who we are not, or what we do or do not control. After all, as children of God, we can boast of nothing outside of Christ. We are who we are in Him. We can do all things through Him. In Him we live and move and have our being.

Let us humble ourselves before God daily, especially when we are praised for "our" accomplishments. We have nothing of real value that we did not receive. There can be no big fall, if we never climb a high wall.

I will daily humble myself before God. When others give me praise for the things I do, I will return the praise to Him, because He is the source of my supply.

Day 140
Hebrews 4:16

"Let us therefore come boldly before the throne of grace, that we may obtain mercy, and find grace to help in the time of need."

Hebrews 4:16 lets us know the kind of attitude we should have when we approach God in a time of need. We should come expecting to obtain mercy and find grace to help us. Our degree of hesitancy or confidence reveals the state of our relationship with God and the level of our faith in His Word.

Our goal is to come boldly. When we come boldly, we have confidence and are not afraid of being rebuked or denied. The verse said we should come boldly to obtain something. So, we must release faith. Faith is based upon a knowing. That knowing comes from an understanding of the Word of God and a relationship with God that gives us confidence in His integrity.

We can monitor how we are growing in our relationship with the Father, as we see how bold we are before the throne of grace. Let us press toward the mark of knowing Him so well, that it does not ever occur to us that we might not get what we need when we approach Him. Let us grow to the place where we go with excitement, knowing that He knows what our need is and looks forward to meeting it. At that point, we will probably find ourselves bypassing asking and just thanking Him in advance, knowing that He takes pleasure in giving us what we need and more.

I will grow in my relationship with God, until I have such confidence in Him, that I approach Him boldly, thanking Him in advance for all I know He will do.

Day 141
John 15:14

"You are my friends if you do what I command."

Jesus wants us to be His friends. He said His friends are those who obey His commands. Since He gives commands, He must want us to obey them. Since He wants obedience, and obedience creates friendship, He must want friends.

Are we His friends? How intimate is our friendship? Are we casual friends, who are occasionally obedient or are we close friends who are always obedient? Can He always depend on us? It is up to us how deep our friendship will go. He has given us His commands in the Bible and continues to speak to us by His Spirit. We choose how much we want to obey.

Let us examine where we are and how far we want to go and behave ourselves accordingly. It is amazing how much more fulfilling our lives can be when we become consumed with doing the Master's will. It will become impossible to be depressed and give up. Though it may present itself, we will not have enough idle time to allow depression to get a grip. We become people of purpose and destiny. Better than that, we become His friends.

I will increase in my obedience to Christ. I will become a close friend of His.

Day 142
Romans 8:12

"Therefore, brethren, we are debtors, not to the flesh, to live after the flesh."

It can be a relief to us if we comprehend what Paul is saying in Romans 8:12. It may come as a surprise to most Christians that we do not owe our flesh anything. The only thing we can be sure it has done for us is cause trouble. So, why do we struggle when our flesh is tempted to do wrong?

If someone who has been nothing but a "pain" asks us to do something out of order, we probably would not struggle over whether or not we will cooperate. If they beg and plead, we may not feel we owe it to them to respond affirmatively, especially when it will probably get us in trouble. So why do we struggle with, and sometimes give in to the flesh, when it will hurt us?

The struggle is mainly a result of misunderstanding. We are three-part beings. We are spirits that have souls and live in bodies. Our spirits are supposed to be in charge. We need our souls and bodies to function on our planet. They assist the spirit. Some people do not know the distinction between the three parts. They have become confused at times about who is in charge and have responded without a clear understanding of what they were doing. Others are aware of the difference, but have not allowed the Word of God to saturate their hearts and minds to a point of a clear separation. They have responded to the flesh out of habit before they were fully aware of their illogical behavior.

If we will strengthen our spirits and train our souls (mind, will and emotion) with the Word of God on a consistent basis, we will be better able to stand up to our flesh when temptation arises. Romans 8:12 helps us understand the attitude we should take when dealing with the flesh. With this attitude, we should speak aloud to our flesh and "straighten it out." The more we grow close to God and desire to please Him totally, the easier it will be to speak up to the flesh and say, "It doesn't matter to me how you feel or how bad you want to do that. I don't owe you anything. You serve me. I don't serve you. I am under authority, and I take orders from Heaven. You will take orders from me! Now here's what we will do."

I do not owe my flesh anything. I will not serve it. It will serve me. We will glorify our Lord and Savior, Jesus Christ.

Day 143
Judges 6:17

"And he said unto him, If now I have found grace in thy sight, then show me a sign that thou talkest with me."

In Judges 6, Gideon communicated with an angel who came on God's behalf to inform him of a divine assignment. Gideon was not accustomed to hearing from God, and therefore needed a sign to help him believe. In that chapter, Gideon received three signs to reassure him that God had spoken to him and would help him with his assignment.

Like Gideon, all of us had to begin somewhere in our relationship with God. The less we knew Him, the more we needed signs. As we grow in our personal relationship with the Lord, we will need signs less frequently to perform His will.

Gideon said, "If now I have found grace." He was not sure of God's favor (His willingness to use His power on Gideon's behalf) towards him. Asking for signs and waiting for confirmations exposes our level of relationship. Regardless of where we are, we should strive to grow closer to God by spending more time with him, so our confidence can increase.

Paul said, "I know whom I have believed and am persuaded that he is able to keep that which I have committed unto him." He also said, "That I may know Him." He had increased in knowing God, which increased his confidence, but he realized there was still room to grow.

God can use all of us. However, the more our confidence in Him increases, the more useful we will be to the kingdom of God. We can be available to do more things on short notice when we do not need a sign for every instruction. We can go places others are afraid to go, because of our assurance that God's grace is with us.

I will draw closer to God and increase my confidence in His favor toward me. I will need signs or confirmation less and less, as I know Him more and more.

Day 144
Numbers 23:3

"And Balaam said unto Balak, Stand by thy burnt offering, and I will go: peradventure the Lord will come to meet me: and whatsoever he sheweth me, I will tell thee..."

One important lesson we must learn is that of strict obedience. Balaam said he would report precisely what he was shown. Because we do not understand all God tells us, we can always be tempted to alter the instructions we receive from Him. Sometimes our disobedience can be the result of pride or fear. We can also attempt to adjust what we have heard so it will make sense to us. In whatever way the temptation may come to alter God's Word, we must resist it. If we were following a recipe, assembly instructions, or directions to a particular location, one modification could cause a small problem, or it could mean disaster.

Let us think for a moment about the kind of relationship we would want to have with a person who, from time to time, without notice, alters our instructions. Although we may be merciful and patient, we would not look to give them an assignment of great importance. We would only try to use them on minor projects.

Strict obedience comes through spiritual growth and practice. We must dictate to our flesh and not vice versa. The next time God instructs us, let us remember the words of Mary in John 2:5, "Whatsoever he saith unto you, do it."

I will, with God's help, practice and walk in strict obedience to God's instructions. I am obedient.

Day 145
Numbers 23:19

"God is not a man that he should lie; neither the son of man, that he should repent: hath he said, and shall he not do it? Or hath he spoken, and shall he not make it good?"

In Numbers 23, Balaam prophesied, as God directed him. As he spoke, he declared a difference between God and man. Man can lie, but God cannot. That is an extremely important fact.

Sometimes people, in an attempt to explain what they do not understand, blame everything on God. They may say God is sovereign and He has a purpose for everything. These people generally do not recognize the authority God gave man, or the activity of Satan. They also do not recognize God's integrity. Whether good or evil, pleasant or unpleasant, the responsibility is usually placed on God for all of it.

We should be glad that God is sovereign. This means He is supreme in power and authority. We should also be glad He has given His Word and cannot lie. That is the only way we can know what is of God and what is not. He said in Psalm 89:34 that He will not alter what He has said. So we can trust Him.

If God was totally mysterious and we never knew what He was going to do, it would be difficult to know Him or trust Him. Trust is based on a knowledge of current facts. Thank God He does not change. The facts about Him are always current. What He said, He will do. What He spoke, He will make good. How comforting it is to be able to go to His Word in a time of need, knowing that it is always dependable. Our faith can grow exceedingly, as we meditate the Word with this understanding.

I will remind myself of God's integrity and build my faith with His Word daily.

Day 146
Numbers 23:20

"Behold, I have received commandment to bless: and he hath blessed; and I cannot reverse it."

God gave the commandment to bless, and then He performed the blessing. In his prophecy concerning Israel, Balaam spoke forth what God had done. There was no way out of it. The Lord initiated it and then confirmed it. He is determined to bless His people. The prophet said, "I cannot reverse it."

Once again, the scripture is clear about God's attitude toward His own. We are the only ones who can reverse our blessings, because we are the recipients. We can receive or reject them. We can cooperate with God and walk in what He has provided, or we can rebel and hence, remove ourselves from the path of blessing.

One way we can reverse our blessing is by attributing the work of Satan to God. When the enemy attacks and we receive it as punishment, God's teaching or working our ultimate good, we blaspheme against God and deny His blessing. When we resist the enemy, God's blessing produces victory over him. However, when we do not realize who our enemy is, we cannot resist him. Instead, we assist him.

No one, not even Satan, can reverse our blessing. Once God has blessed, it is final with Him. Our failure to receive it does not change anything from God's end. Knowing this can deliver us, because if we wake up to truth, we can reverse the curse we may have opened the door to in our lives. We can do this, because the blessing is still in effect. We can rise up, resist the devil, and he will flee from us. Then, with the words of our mouths, we can declare that we receive the blessings of God that belong to us.

I reverse the curse and receive the irreversible blessing God has pronounced on me.

Day 147
Numbers 23:21

"He hath not beheld iniquity in Jacob, neither hath he seen perverseness in Israel: the Lord his God is with him, and the shout of a king is among them."

By the time this prophecy was spoken, the children of Israel had provoked God to anger many times. It is amazing that He found no fault with them. What a merciful, gracious and forgiving God we serve! He removes our sins from us as far as the east is from the west. He remembers them no more.

Once Israel had repented and followed God's requirements to cover their sin, it was over. All they had was the blood of cattle and types of shadows of Jesus, yet God beheld them blameless. How much more, then, will He see us faultless who have been washed in the blood of His son! When we obey God and repent of our sins, we must accept God's forgiveness and restoration to right standing. As we see in Numbers 23:21, the way God sees us spiritually affects our victory. Because He did not find fault with Israel at that time, He was ready to fight for them, and there was no chance they would lose.

"The shout of a king," the verse said, "is among them." That meant victory in this case, because the context is war, and God was on their side. A king never shouts meaninglessly. When a king shouts, there is either reason to celebrate, or something else is about to change. According to Revelation 1:6, Jesus has made us kings unto God. Since He is on our side, guaranteeing us victory, from time to time we ought to hear ourselves shout the victory.

Let us rejoice in our great salvation. Let us show gratitude and appreciation to our Heavenly Father, who has shown such great loving kindness and tender mercies toward us. Jude 24 and 25 says, "Now unto him that is able to keep you from falling, and to present you faultless before the presence of his glory with exceeding joy, To the only wise God and Savior, be glory and majesty, dominion and power, both now and ever. Amen."

I will appreciate and be grateful to God for His great mercy and grace. I will celebrate the guaranteed victory He has given me and shout like a king.

Day 148
Numbers 23:22

"God brought them out of Egypt; he hath as it were the strength of an unicorn."

Egypt, which was a type of the kingdom of darkness, was a place the Israelites were never to return to. Numbers 23:22 says, "God brought them out of Egypt." Israel's deliverance from their place of slavery was a very significant event. It is mentioned in this prophetic passage, because it represented the supreme, unmatchable power of the Almighty God.

We must meditate on our deliverance from the kingdom of darkness, until we appreciate just how dynamic an event it was. It was a demonstration of God's sharing with us His power to overcome. He enabled us to defy all the power of our enemy and come through unharmed.

We must meditate on our deliverance from Satan's kingdom, until we would never be foolish enough to return to it or even look back. By a mighty hand, God has brought us out. The power He gave us to leave the kingdom of darkness is the power we have to remain in the Kingdom of Light.

God brought me out of darkness into His marvelous light. I appreciate that. The power of the Holy Spirit that has brought me out will keep me strong and firmly planted in the Kingdom of Light.

Day 149

Numbers 23:23

"Surely there is no enchantment against Jacob, neither is there any divination against Israel: according to this time it shall be said of Jacob and Israel, What hath God wrought!"

During the time when Baalam was asked to curse Israel, the world was full of all kinds of idol worship. Witchcraft and other forms of the occult were common. When the king of Moab asked Baalam to curse the children of Israel, he did not understand that he had not only come against Israel, but also the Almighty God. There was no enchantment against God, who was on their side.

We must stay in fellowship with God and walk in confidence, free from fear of any contrary powers. Jesus said, "All power is given unto me in heaven and in earth." If God has all power, then there is none left for anyone else, including Satan. Any power that Satan or any human being has is null and void in the presence of God. If we ever think someone is attempting to harm us in any way, including using witchcraft, we should boldly declare our protection from all power that is not of God.

Isaiah 54:17 declares that the servants of God have victory over every weapon formed against them. It says they have the right to condemn every word spoken against them. Our enemy has already been conquered for us. We are responsible to enforce that defeat. Just like it happened with Israel, after all the enemy's attempts, people will be able to look at us and say, "Look at what the Lord has done!"

No evil can work against me. I am eternally victorious. I stand firm in my freedom from the powers of darkness. God is on my side, and others will look at me and say, "Look what the Lord has done!"

Day 150
Numbers 23:24

"Behold, the people shall rise up as a great lion, and lift up himself as a young lion: he shall not lie down until he eat of the prey, and drink the blood of the slain."

Look at how God not only declared victory for His people, but how he also bragged on them. Numbers 23:24 expresses the way God looks at us and expects us to act.

We must rise up with confidence like great lions. We must pick ourselves up on the inside, like young lions who do not intend to stop their fight until they have conquered. We should envision victory before we get started. Let us see the end from the beginning, realizing our victory before the fight begins. When we do this, we will not quit until we are finished – until we taste the victory.

I will not fight with "maybes" in my mind. I will win, and I will win big. I will not quit until I experience the victory paid for by God, my father. I am more than a conqueror through Jesus Christ.

Day 151
Proverbs 12:13

"The wicked is snared by the transgression of his lips; but the just shall come out of trouble."

Some of us, or maybe all of us, have had a particular spiritual test more than once. We have failed miserably in the way we handled it, and before too long, we got another chance to see how we would fare. Solomon said in Proverbs 12:13, "The wicked is snared by the transgression of his lips." It is not just because of his wickedness that a person gets into trouble, but his wickedness comes through his mouth and causes the trouble. If he would say the right things, he could save himself. The same is true for us, the righteous. The verse above states, "the just shall come out of trouble." It is not only because he is just that he is delivered, but his righteousness comes from his lips and saves him. Either he speaks out of his faith toward God, or he calls on God for help.

In times past, we have been trapped in the same way the wicked have brought hurt to themselves – by wrong reactions to our trouble. We have uttered the wrong words. Our self control was overridden by our desire to serve our flesh for a moment. Our behavior exemplified that of someone who has no hope, or no God. Our test grade was 'F' that time. If we are realistic, we know another opportunity will come to pass the same test again. So, we need to make preparations. We need to study and condition ourselves to prepare for success. We have what it takes. God will not allow us to experience a test that is too difficult for us to pass. However, He will not do our homework for us or guarantee our success, without our having to do our part.

As we study, let us meditate on how we should have responded. How would Jesus have responded? If we already knew the right response, we must question why the wrong reaction was manifested. If our flesh was dominating at the time, we need to restructure our time to feed our spirits more than our flesh. We may need to allocate more time to prayer, Bible study or declarations of God's word. Or, perhaps we only need to give one area in particular more attention. Whatever the case, may we be better prepared when the test comes around again.

I will fortify myself to be able to pass the tests I have failed. By the help of God, I will overcome and glorify my Lord by the manner in which I conduct myself.

Day 152
Matthew 2:2

"Saying, where is he that is born King of the Jews? For we have seen his star in the east, and are come to worship him."

Nearly 2,000 years ago, some men who studied the stars (possibly astronomers and astrologers) came to Jerusalem in search of a king they believed was born there. They were led in their search by an unusual star in the east. We cannot be certain how far they came from, but we know they traveled for some time, because their journey began about two years before they arrived in Jerusalem. If they began following the star several months after it had appeared, they would still have been traveling for several months. According to Matthew's account, these men were so confident they would find the young king, that they brought gifts of gold, frankincense and myrrh, and asked, "Where is he?" They did not ask if a king had been born. They asked where he was.

This story is a lesson to us about faith. To what extreme will, we go if we really believe what we say we believe? Because the seekers from the east were so confident, they left their homes and traveled for a long time to discover what they were sure they would find. People sometimes make sacrifices for things they are not sure of. Hope alone drives people to extremes.

How, then, do we explain the faith of those who say they are convinced and make no effort to find or accomplish anything?

The confident expectation of the woman with the abnormal bleeding condition caused her to ignore the rules of society and press through a crowd to touch the hem of Jesus' garment. Four men believed Jesus could raise up their friend. Their belief caused them to climb a roof and let him down through the tiling where the Master could get to him.

It is important that we realize the need to increase our faith by hearing God's Word and acting on it on a consistent basis. As James said, faith is demonstrated by works, not just words. When our faith is strong, we will not just talk about it, but we will also show it. Until we can "put our money where our mouths are," let us be slow to speak around others about what we believe, and speak mostly to God and ourselves, as we build <u>real</u> faith.

I will measure my faith by my works. I will hear and act on God's Word and build strong faith continually. My faith will be seen by my performance.

Day 153
Psalm 60:12

"*Through God we shall do valiantly: for he it is that shall tread down our enemies.*"

It is ***through God*** that we can do all things. Through ***God*** we overcome every obstacle, defeat every enemy and accomplish every impossible task. Paul said in Philippians 4:13 (J.B.Phillips translation), "I am ready for anything through the strength of the One who lives within me." That is why we must develop a God consciousness. When we are constantly aware of God's presence, we are invincible. As we set out to fulfill His will for our lives, He provides the tools necessary to accomplish every task.

The Psalmist said, "For it is he that shall tread down our enemies." Paul said in I Corinthians 3:9, "For we are laborers together with God." This is not our show. We are performers in a drama written and directed by someone else. It is not up to us to provide the props or other necessary things or even to determine the outcome. We simply need to read our lines and follow the instructions of the director, who knows the end from the beginning. Our Father does not produce failures. We can only fail if we write our own lines and choose our own plan of action.

So, let us stay with God. It is through Him that we shall do valiantly. For as we labor with Him, He will tread down our enemies, as He goes before us and prepares the way for His plan to be accomplished.

I am a laborer with God. I will cooperate with His plan and follow the script He has written for me. Through my God, I shall do valiantly. It is He who will tread down my enemies. I see nothing but victory ahead.

Day 154
Psalm 103:1

"Bless the Lord, O my soul: and all that is within me, bless his holy name."

The psalmist David considered God to be so great, that he wanted to bless him with all he had. We may have sung the song, "Bless the Lord, O my soul," and thought of verbal praise to God. However, we can take it a step further and consider our actions on a daily basis as opportunities to bless the Lord with our lives.

Colossians 3:24 says, "And whatsoever ye do, do it heartily, as to the Lord, and not to men." Our lives should bless the Lord, as we seek to honor Him in everything we do. The words of our mouths and the meditation of our hearts should bless Him. Our actions should bless Him, as we do those things that are pleasing in His sight.

We can take it a step further by commanding our bodies to function properly, as God designed them to. As we do our part to take care of our bodies, which are God's temples, our limbs, organs, tissues and cells – all that is within us, should bless the Lord, by functioning in perfection.

As we speak, act and live healthy and whole as unto the Lord, we can bless Him with our souls and all that is within us. Let us start thinking more like this today, and may the song, "Bless the Lord, O my soul," take on new meaning for us and become more meaningful to God as we sing it.

I will bless the Lord with my soul and all that is within me today. I will speak and act in a way that will bless Him. I will command my body to function in a manner that will bless Him. I <u>will</u> bless the Lord.

Day 155
Ephesians 4:28

"Let him that stole steal no more: but rather let him labor, working with his hands the thing which is good, that he may have to give to him that needeth."

In Ephesians 4:28, Paul said the man who is a thief should not just stop stealing, but he should begin giving. Stealing comes from selfishness. Practicing giving will replace the selfishness and strengthen us against the temptation to steal again. When we are set free from one thing, we are delivered to something else. We move from stealing to giving, from being bound to setting others free, from hating to loving, and so on.

We are blessed to be a blessing. God wants us to receive, so we can have something to give. When we cease to function in our purpose for being delivered, we can backslide into the bondage we came from. Jesus said when an evil spirit leaves, if he comes and finds that his previous place has not been occupied, he will re-enter, bringing more wicked spirits with him. Refraining from doing bad things is not good enough. We must be constantly doing good.

Jesus taught us to forgive. He said prayer should be offered for those who mistreat us. When we forgive, we replace bitterness with love, as we bless those who curse us and pray for those who hurt us. If we do not do something positive to replace the wrong feelings that came to us when we were offended, it can prolong our healing from the pain. It can also make repeating the offense more likely. We do not have to jeopardize our safety to do something positive for an enemy. However, we must be careful to do something. If nothing else is appropriate, praying for that person will suffice. Then, we can be led by the Spirit of God, if there is anything else to be done.

When we were saved, we were delivered from selfishness. We gave up everything at that moment, as we surrendered our entire lives to Christ. Shortly after that, the temptation came again for us to selfishly run our lives. If we became regular church attendees at a place where the Word of God was taught, we most likely received help in replacing bad habits with good ones. If we began reading our Bibles and praying, that should have helped us. Satan will continue to test us to see how selfishly he can get us to live again. He will encourage us to look out for ourselves first and always try to have things our own way. If we are going to stay on top, we must not only refrain from evil, but we must also practice doing good.

Let us look around today and see what we have to give to someone in need. We can probably think of things we have had around for years, like clothing, furniture, etc., that we have planned to use, but somehow have never gotten around to it. These are things we have to give. Let us do it. If someday we were to decide we could have used the things we gave away, we will be in a position to get them again. God gives seed to the sower and multiplies the seed sown. We will reap what we sow.

I will practice giving. I have received things to be able to give. I am blessed to be a blessing.

Day 156
I Peter 2:24

"Who his own self bare our sins in his own body on the tree, that we, being dead to sins, should live unto righteousness: by whose stripes ye were healed."

Jesus went through a lot to provide salvation for us. As I Peter 2:24 reveals, He took care of our sins and sickness on the cross. As we think back on Calvary, let us appreciate and appropriate all that was provided.

Our Savior set His face to go to Jerusalem one day. It took dedication, determination, and great love to finish the course of redeeming mankind. He was betrayed by a man he loved. Judas worked with Him for three years, during which time Jesus met all his needs. Then, for thirty pieces of silver, he betrayed his master. His other disciples fled, when He was arrested. Peter and John stayed close by to see what would become of Him. Then, Peter denied knowing Him, for fear of what it might cost him, if they found out he was one of the twelve who served Christ faithfully. Ashamed of what he had done, Peter wept bitterly, as he left the scene. John was the only disciple of the twelve who remained close by until the end to see what would become of the Son of God.

Jesus was dragged before unjust men and tried as a criminal in a court that was unfair. He was mocked, badly beaten and humiliated, as they spat on Him. Foreign soldiers beat His back 39 times with a whip, ripping open his flesh. A crown of thorns was placed on His head, and blood flowed all over His body. He was made to carry a cross up Golgotha's hill. After He fell under the load of that cross, someone else had to carry the tree the rest of the way. Then, they nailed his hands and feet to the cross. The sinners He was dying to save helped carry out the sentence upon this just Man. He prayed for their forgiveness, as He prepared to breathe His last breath as a human being.

Matthew 27:46 records his agonizing cry to His Father, "My God, my God, why hast thou forsaken me?" For the first time, He experienced the horrible separation from God that He came to deliver man from. As Jesus took upon Himself the sin of the world, God had to turn away from His only begotten Son.

He spent three days and nights in Hell and took the punishment we would have received, so we would never have to experience it. Then, when justice was served and the price was paid for our sin, He officially defeated the powers of darkness and loosed the Old Testament saints, who were waiting for Him in a place called "Abraham's Bosom." He was resurrected. He returned to Heaven and placed His blood on the mercy seat to begin a new era for humanity. The blood represents His successful venture to make a way for man to be free of Satan's power and live eternally with God.

He took our sins, so we could have His righteousness. He bore our sicknesses and diseases, so we could enjoy health. When someone works hard to give us something, if we really want to make them feel like everything they went through was worth it, we would tell them how we used the gift and how much it helped. Let us express gratitude, as we receive and walk by faith in the benefits provided for us.

I receive what God has provided for me through Jesus Christ. By faith, I will walk in my salvation. I am free from sin and sickness and disease.

Day 157
Psalm 18:1

"I will love thee, O Lord, my strength."

In Psalm 18:1, the declaration of David, the psalmist, was an intelligent one. He was not just saying he would love

God who was his strength, and on whom he was taught to depend. He knew the Lord to be his strength by experience.

When we hear that we can rely on God to be our strength, we may call on Him in time of trouble, because of what we have heard about Him. When we experience Him as our strength, it makes a difference when we call on Him again. In Romans 5:4, Paul tells us that experience brings hope. Hope is an image we have, based on facts. When we are told something by someone credible, we consider it factual information. We can create an image, based on their words. Once we have had an experience for ourselves, that image becomes more vivid. Since faith is released because of hope, it is easier to release faith when our hope is stronger. Our hope can be stronger after personal experience.

The more we experience the Lord as our strength, the more we will be able to say what David said, "I will love you, O Lord, my strength." Just like someone would say to another who has helped them tremendously, "I love you, my helper," so we will say to God, "I love you, my Strength." These are not just words. It is an emotional response out of gratitude for the relationship that has been so beneficial. The experience we have with God should increase our appreciation and love for Him.

I will release faith based upon the hope I have. My faith will produce experiences that will increase my hope. My increased hope will enable me to release my faith and have more experiences. Out of gratitude to God, I will express my love and appreciation for each and every experience we enjoy together. My love and appreciation for the Lord is increasing continually.

Day 158
Genesis 1:1

"In the beginning God created the heaven and the earth."

From time to time, it is important that we remind ourselves of some basic things about God. One of those things is that He is the Creator of heaven and earth. He owns it all. He was big enough to do it alone. He is that intelligent. His creativity is awesome. His desire for beauty and his ability to produce it is obvious.

As we meditate on the attributes of God which are revealed through His creation and remind ourselves that He is our Father, who is willing to be actively involved in our lives, it can affect our productivity. We can have a more positive outlook. Sometimes, we allow fear and helplessness to overtake us, as we limit ourselves to our natural resources. The more we meditate on God through the Word and praise and worship him, the less we will find ourselves limited by fear or a sense of helplessness.

Let us take time to notice creation today and respond to God, based on what we see. As a result of what we see, we can praise and worship Him and thank Him for being our Help every day.

I will observe creation today and remind myself about who God is. My Father created Heaven and earth. He is great, and He is my God. I will praise and worship Him.

Day 159
Isaiah 60:2

"For, behold, the darkness shall cover the earth, and gross darkness the people: but the Lord shall arise upon thee, and His glory shall be seen upon thee."

God never promised that darkness would leave the earth and remain absent until the end of time. As long as man has the ability to choose and evil is available, there will be darkness. Jesus warned us that wickedness would increase towards the end of the age. The apostle Paul spoke of evil men becoming worse and worse during the last days. However, as Isaiah prophesied, there is a bright side for God's people. No matter how dark it is, there is victory for us. We are the light of the world.

It is difficult to tell that a flashlight is shining outdoors at high noon. The darker it gets however, the easier it is to see light. Light is more powerful than darkness. Light can always expel darkness. Darkness cannot overpower light. Light has to be turned off for it to become so bright that darkness disappears.

So, on one hand, we can be saddened, as we see such darkness covering our land. On the other hand, we can realize that there has never been a better time to invade the darkness, because light shows up better in darkness. Isaiah 60:3 says, "And the Gentiles shall come to thy light, and kings to the brightness of thy rising." As we allow the glory of God to be seen upon us, the lost who want help will not be able to miss us. Wherever we shine, we will be seen, and they shall come to Christ.

Let us take advantage today of opportunities to promote the light of the gospel of Christ. We can shine by our words and actions. We can give financial and physical support to those who are using various means to spread the gospel. Our prayers can make a difference. The opportunity to reach the lost is great. The darkness should not discourage us, but rather move us to action.

I will be encouraged today by opportunities to spread the gospel of Jesus Christ. I will take advantage of whatever means I find to help light the way for those in darkness who desire freedom.

Day 160
Ezra 6:8

"Moreover I make a decree what ye shall do to the elders of these Jews for the building of this house of God: that of the king's goods, even of the tribute beyond the river, forthwith expenses be given unto these men, that they be not hindered."

Ezra recorded the story of how the temple of God was rebuilt after the children of Israel were taken into captivity. The Lord moved upon the heart of King Cyrus to make sure the temple was constructed. The king provided all that was needed to get the job done. He gave specific instructions, so everyone would understand that he sanctioned the project and no one would hinder them.

God is awesome. This story shows us how God possesses the wealth of the world and has the power to distribute it as He pleases. However, we see that He works through people. Someone from among His people had to have a desire to see the job done. So, God found someone to work through to supply the need. It did not matter if the person He found was a king who did not have a covenant with God. All King Cyrus had belonged to God anyway.

We should never be envious of the wicked or of unbelievers who have great possessions. When we are faithful over little, God will make us ruler over much, even if he has to stir up the ungodly to give it to us. The Lord gives seed to sowers. The faithful man abounds with blessings. As we do the things necessary to posses the wealth of the world, including getting our words and actions in line with God's will, we will take what belongs to us for the glory of God.

I will do what is necessary, as the Holy Spirit guides me, to possess the wealth God wants to give me to make me a greater blessing. This is my Father's world. I will not live in lack while I am here.

Day 161
Hosea 6:3 Amplified Version

"Yes, let us know – recognize, be acquainted with and understand him; let us be zealous to know the Lord – to appreciate, give heed to and cherish him. His going forth is prepared and certain as the dawn, and He will come to us as the [heavy] rains, as the latter rain that waters the earth."

God already knows everything about us. As the prophet Hosea said, we need to know Him. The exhortation in Hosea 6:3 encourages us to get acquainted with God and be zealous about it, because we need to appreciate and cherish Him. It is to our advantage to follow Him in strict obedience, and the more we know and understand Him, the easier it will be to obey Him.

The scripture said, "His going forth is prepared and certain as the dawn." It may be surprising to us as humans to find that someone we thought we knew has changed. We should not be concerned, however, that God will change. We will never experience getting to know Him, and then one day discover He has suddenly changed. He never changes. He said He will never desert us and He never will. He said He is our Healer. He always will be. When things are not going the way they should, there is no need to see if God has changed His mind. He never does. We should just examine ourselves and press on for more understanding.

When we begin to feel that God is not as close to us as He once was, He has not moved. <u>We</u> need to make the adjustment, if one needs to be made, or accept by faith that all is well. If we are not enjoying the peace Jesus said He left for us, He has not taken it back. We must find out what we did with it.

Let us examine ourselves today to see where we are with God. Our state of mind can help us determine if we need to pursue Him a little harder. We should pursue, not as if we are running after someone, but rather to close the distance between us and someone we have strayed away from, or want to be closer to.

I will make adjustments and pursue getting closer to God today. I will be zealous to know, appreciate, cherish and be obedient to Him. He is my constant, eternal friend.

Day 162
Psalm 97:1

"The Lord reigneth; let the earth rejoice; let the multitude of the isles be glad thereof."

The psalmist announced that the multitude of the islands can be glad, because the Lord reigns. When God is in control, there is cause to rejoice. He does all things well.

There is no evil in Heaven, and none will ever be tolerated. God controls Heaven. When Lucifer rebelled, he was immediately kicked out of Heaven. He fell from heaven like lightning.

Man was given dominion over the earth. As long as he submitted to God, everything was perfect. It was when he submitted to Satan that all the ills and woes in this world began. When the period of man's rule on earth is over, the Lord will reign on the earth for one thousand years, and there will be peace and a wonderful life for all.

When God is in control of our lives, everything turns out right. It is easy to tell when we have taken over. Chaos and frustration fills our atmosphere, and we feel like climbing the walls after a while. Then we cry out to God and surrender to Him. When we do this, He brings order and peace, and we are so glad He was there to take over.

We can understand why the psalmist said, "The Lord reigneth, let the earth rejoice." Let us work today through every means we have to support His taking over our neighborhoods, cities, states, countries and world. May we allow Him to take charge of our lives also. When God is in control, everyone can be happy, for that is His goal. He wants mankind to serve Him with gladness and joy.

I will contribute to God's running the entire world. I will begin by giving Him charge of my life everyday.

Day 163
Colossians 4:13 NIV

"I vouch for him that he is working hard for you and for those at Laodicea and Hierapolis."

Paul wrote to the saints at Colossee about a man named Epaphras. He told them Epaphras prayed fervently for them to become stable and fully matured. Paul confirmed that this intercessor was sincere. For Paul to vouch for him, he had to have evidence of Epaphras' zeal.

What will our husbands, wives, children or other family members say, as they affirm things about us that are undeniable? Will our coworkers vouch for us about things we will be proud of? How about those we work for, or work with in ministry? May our lives today add to a reputation we can be proud of. When they say, "One thing for sure I can tell you about him or her is...," may we be able to hold our heads up and smile. May we be able to give God the glory, because of what we have allowed Him to do through us.

Father, In Jesus name, help me today to be aware that all I do will add to what is said about me. What is said can give me an opportunity to give you glory, when this day is done. I will lift up my head in praise to you, because of what I have allowed you to do through me. Amen.

Day 164
Psalm 33:1 NIV

"Sing joyfully to the Lord, you righteous; it is fitting for the upright to praise him."

The psalmist encouraged joyful singing to the Lord as an appropriate thing for the ones who served God. He said, "It is fitting for the upright to praise him." There have probably been times when we were arranging items or matching an outfit, and something did not look right. When we made a substitution we were pleased with, we felt relief and satisfaction, as we viewed the situation and saw that everything was perfect. The changes we made were appropriate. The new item or arrangement, was fitting.

Our times of praise to God should increase, because it is fitting. It just looks right. If we see someone outside a church service praising God, our first thought would probably be that

God had done something for them. We would assume they are a believer. But, if we found that person was wicked, (not a wicked person who was repenting), we would possibly be annoyed, thinking they were mocking God. Praising God does not fit the ungodly, although there are occasions when they may do so sincerely. We may even react in disgust in church to see an obvious hypocrite praising God, if we thought they were not sincere. It just seems that people praising God should be sincere persons who are living upright or, at least experiencing a change in their lives that would cause them to do so.

Psalm 107:1-2 NIV says, "Give thanks unto the Lord, for he is good; his love endures forever. Let the redeemed of the Lord say this – those he redeemed from the hand of the foe." It just seems to be the appropriate thing to do. When we have gone a long time without praising God, we just do not look right. Let us check up on our praise life the next time it seems that something is out of order. It may be the very adjustment we need to make.

I will check up on myself and make the praise adjustment when necessary. I will practice praising God more and more, until I always look right.

Day 165
Psalm 33:18,19

"Behold, the eye of the Lord is upon them that fear him, upon them that hope in his mercy;
To deliver their soul from death, and to keep them alive in famine."

Do we hear the Word of the Lord through the psalmist? If we listen carefully and allow our spirits and minds to absorb what the Spirit of God is saying, our faith will be boosted, and our fears will scatter.

The eye of the Lord is upon them that fear Him. God's eye does not miss anything. It is constantly on those who fear Him and hope in His mercy. All who reverence God and realize the need for His mercy and depend on it will not be disappointed. God not only watches them, but He also watches them to deliver them. He delivers them from death and enables them to survive in the midst of famine. Our Father makes a way for us all the time. He sees everything and watches with a purpose. He takes excellent care of what belongs to Him.

Let us make sure we stay in a position to receive God's deliverance and care. We must continually reverence Him, meaning we should be obedient with a positive attitude. Then, we must believe in His mercy and look for it.

I will reverence the Lord at all times. I will believe in and look for His mercy.

Day 166

Deuteronomy 7:15

"And the Lord will take away from thee all sickness, and will put none of the evil diseases of Egypt, which thou knowest, upon thee; but will lay them upon all them that hate thee."

In this passage, God was speaking to the nation of Israel through Moses, to inform them of what they were to expect when they walked in their covenant. As a part of this covenant, God would permit diseases to come upon their enemies and would remove all diseases from them.

This is a very important lesson for us. We see what God's will is for us relative to our health. As we walk in the way

He has ordained for us, we are supposed to walk free of malfunctions in our bodies. When we see sickness or disease come upon our bodies, our attitude should be alarm. Our question should be, "What is the disease of the ungodly doing on my body?" It should be our aim to get rid of the curse that God did not ordain for His people.

Jeremiah 33:3 says, "Call unto me, and I will answer thee, and shew thee great and mighty things, which thou knowest not." James 1:5 says, "If any of you lack wisdom, let him ask of God, that giveth to all men liberally, and upbraideth not; and it shall be given him."

The above scriptures let us know that there are times when we need understanding and insight that can help us. We should seek God, not in fear, but in faith. God can answer us in different ways, so we may sometimes need to wait a while for our response. We must, however, expect an answer. Until we see the desired result, our attitude should be positive. We should go about our Father's business cheerfully, believing that every wrong thing will be made right. In other words, we must wait in faith.

It is very important that we see things the way God sees them. If we do not, we can suffer unnecessarily. God sees sickness and disease as something that should not be on His people. Regardless of what we see, let us agree with God and work to help ourselves and our brothers experience the perfect will of God - freedom from sickness and disease.

I reject sickness and disease. I trust God for understanding and insight that will help me and others. Sickness and disease do not belong among God's people. I belong to God, and I claim the health He has provided for me.

Day 167
Matthew 2:2

"Saying, Where is he that is born King of the Jews? For we have seen his star in the east, and are come to worship him."

In the second chapter of Matthew, wise men came from the east to see Jesus. They claimed to have seen a star that indicated a king had been born, and they had come to worship him. They came to worship a baby, because of what they saw.

This story helps us understand why we should have no difficulty in worshipping Jesus. It all depends on our vision, or level of understanding. Do we see Him as someone who built us a fire escape to give us an alternative to going to Hell? Do we see a nice, benevolent character, who helps us get our needs met and even gives us what we want sometimes? If that is the extent of what we see when we see Jesus, we will find it difficult to really worship Him. On the other hand, if we see Him as the King of Kings and Lord of Lords, it will be much easier.

Just think about how naturally men react to a high-level dignitary who comes into their presence. Their reaction is different than that to an ordinary citizen, unless they have absolutely no respect for that leader. In some cultures, people stand when a dignitary enters an area. In other places, they bow before the high officials. In any case, there is a reaction, because they recognize the greatness of the person.

God the Father is the Almighty. Jesus Christ is the Son of God, who was made flesh. The Holy Spirit is the third person of the Trinity, who reveals to us the mind of God. By God, manifested in three persons, all creation came in to existence. Genesis 1 and John 1 reveal that the creation of everything on the earth and the creation of mankind was the work of God the Father, Son and Holy Spirit. God is the greatest and highest dignitary in the universe. He is worthy to be worshipped. However, this is not something we understand just by hearing about it. We must have a divine revelation of who He is. A revelation of who God is comes by hearing and understanding. Understanding will come from anointed teaching and personal revelation, as we meditate upon God's Word and fellowship with Him.

May the eyes of our spiritual understanding be enlightened, that we may see the Father, the Son, and the Holy Spirit properly. Then, we will not have to be told to worship Him. Like the wise men from the east, worship will be a reaction to what we see.

I will hear and understand who God is. I will meditate on God's Word and fellowship with Him and thereby know Him more and more. I will worship Him intelligently.

Day 168
Psalm 138:8

"The Lord will perfect that which concerneth me: thy mercy, O Lord, endureth for ever: forsake not the works of thine own hands."

Sometimes it is so easy for us to run our own lives, instead of allowing God to be in control. After all, we manage most of it okay. Without God, of course we would be a successful mess. He causes the sun to shine on the just and the unjust, and were it not for His mercy and loving kindness, all saints and sinners alike would be in a horrible condition. However, because we cannot see Him, we forget that He is responsible for every good and perfect gift in our lives. It may never be revealed in this lifetime how many times he was involved in our accomplishments in inconspicuous ways.

When we understand better how much we need the Lord, we will say what the psalmist, David, said in Psalm 138:8. God's faithfulness to work in our lives is a confession of faith. It is a wonderful reminder to us of how much more progress we can make if we acknowledge Him more. When the full burden for success is on our shoulders, it slows us down and makes us less productive. If, however, we would confess what the psalmist said when it seems we are making no progress, we would see more of the power of God at work in our lives. This applies to changing habits and improving attitudes and character, as well as accomplishing goals.

Let us make David's confession our daily confession, and see how much easier life can be when God is given more control. If we look back and think about some serious improvements that have been made in our lives, we would probably have to say God had obviously helped us. This help could have come through His Word, a chosen vessel, the direct guidance of the Holy Spirit or by some other means.

The Lord is perfecting everything that concerns me. I will remind myself of who is in charge of my life by regularly confessing that the Lord is perfecting whatever concerns me.

Day 169
Ephesians 6:4

"Neither filthiness, nor foolish talking, nor jesting, which are not convenient: but rather giving of thanks."

Jesus had strong exhortations for us about using our mouths. The apostle Paul also made statements, indicating that we should be responsible when it comes to our conversation. In Ephesians 6:4, he puts a priority on thanksgiving, as he commanded the church at Ephesus to refrain from ungodly speech.

There should be no filthy talk among us. Christians should not participate in foolish discussions that are unprofitable, or in vulgar and inappropriate humor that is degrading. We must value our words and use them wisely.

Our speech should give evidence that we are very grateful people. The rule of putting a priority on thanksgiving will eliminate murmuring and complaining. When we focus on giving thanks, realizing we do not do enough of it, it will cause us to humbly show gratitude for the good, instead of emphasizing what is wrong. If we are having difficulty putting up with someone, rather than talking negatively about them, we can be grateful for those who put up with us, including God. Rather than pointing out the faults of those we see, as though we ourselves are free of flaws, we should be grateful that all our shortcomings are not public knowledge.

Gratitude will produce humility. Humility will produce gratitude. They go together. Let us practice including thanksgiving in our speech today. That would include not just saying we are thankful, but demonstrating kindness, as we talk about those we would like to complain about.

An attitude of thanksgiving will dominate my speech. I will increase in humility and gratitude. I am thankful for all God has done for me, directly, and through others.

Day 170
Matthew 7:20

"Wherefore by their fruits ye shall know them."
Jesus taught His disciples to recognize false prophets. He told them they could examine the fruit being produced and

determine who was real, and who was false, who was of God, and who was not of God.

We need to use the same rule, as we judge ourselves. What is the fruit of our doings? There is a difference between having trouble because an evil spirit is opposing us and having trouble because we are causing it. We must be honest and humble, if we are going to stay free of ungodly habits.

Although it can apply to anyone, it is important to note that Jesus was referring to ministers in Matthew 7:20. He said false prophets come in sheep's clothing. That means all appears well. He added, however, that they are like ravening wolves inwardly. In other words, they have ulterior motives, or they minister for their own benefit. He said their fruit will eventually reveal the truth. It is important to note that Jesus is talking about ministers, because we can sometimes justify wrong behavior or attitudes by claiming we are helping others or accomplishing good. Whenever ministry goes forth, people can receive by helping others or accomplishing good. They can receive by faith and be blessed, as God looks upon the heart of those being ministered to. Positive results are not an endorsement of the person or the ministry by God. Jesus once noted that a woman was healed, because of her faith. The anointing of God that was in Him went into the woman, and he did not even know she was there, until He felt the power leave Him. Her receiving was based upon her faith. If He was a prophet who was out of God's will at the time, the woman would still have received her healing.

We must never use positive results to justify ourselves. Let us examine the overall effect of what we are doing. God does not need our help to fulfill His ministry. He needs our cooperation. We should not come up with a plan and ask God's blessing upon it. It is better to wait on God's plan, because it is already blessed. Then, when we think we have His plan, it is important to be open to our having missed it partially or totally. Sometimes, our emotional state at the time can lead us to think we heard from God, when in fact we were led by a desire to fulfill a personal need.

I will be open and honest before God. I will be humble and receive correction relative to the direction I take in my life, especially concerning ministry. I will always be a sheep in sheep's clothing. I will produce only good fruit.

Day 171
Matthew 13:37

"He answered and said unto them, He that soweth the good seed is the Son of man;"

The scripture above was taken from Jesus' explanation of the parable of the wheat and tares. The good seed, which grew up to be wheat, represented the children of the kingdom. The bad seeds were look-alike implants, who were inspired by the devil to dwell among true children of God and cause problems.

It is not God's will that we go on a mission to get rid of the tares. We must follow scriptural patterns and examples. In the gospels, Jesus warned His disciples about imitations of the real thing. In the epistles to the churches, we see leaders warning the flock about false brethren. However, we see noone going on a rampage and developing a ministry that was consumed with getting rid of those in the Body of Christ who were not right.

In an effort to expose and do away with who they supposed to be bad seed, some who have been relentless in attacking ministers have hurt young, or immature believers. They have maybe even hindered some from coming into the Kingdom of God. It may be that even these are evil implants.

We need to be too busy doing our Father's business to have time for a search and destroy mission. Jesus said the servants have been instructed not to attempt to separate the tares and wheat. The removal of the tares will take place at the end of the world, and the job will be given to angels, not to men. With that knowledge, we can relieve ourselves of the burden of what we should do about people in the church who seem to be complete hypocrites. It is necessary that we teach people to recognize false brethren and warn them, as the apostles did, of those who can harm them or threaten their faith. We must not, however, go further than the examples set before us.

Our Lord Jesus has planted us, the good seed, in the world. Let us realize that it is an honor that he has planted us here. It should not be taken lightly. The main purpose of a seed is to reproduce and bring forth fruit. May we be about our master's business today.

I will relieve myself of any burden about false brethren, who have been planted to cause trouble. I will do what I have been taught to do in the Word about that and move right along, reproducing and bearing fruit. I will give thanks today for the honor of being planted by the Lord Jesus Christ in this world. I will endeavor to show my gratitude by doing His will today.

Day 172
Micah 7:8

Rejoice not against me, O mine enemy: when I fall, I shall arise; when I sit in darkness, the Lord shall be a light unto me."

The prophet, Micah, was called by God to prophesy against people who had gone astray from the will of God. He also had a message of hope for the oppressed. He is the one who told of the birthplace of the Messiah, who would bring peace to

His people. In Micah 7:8, the prophet tells the enemy not to get thrilled over the downfall of the people of God, because God will never leave His own in that state.

The apostle Paul referred to God as the God of hope. One reason is because of His faithfulness. As long as we trust in Him, there is hope that no matter what has befallen us, we will rise again. Proverbs 24:16 tells us that a just man gets back up after falling seven times. Micah said, "When I sit in darkness, the Lord shall be a light unto me." The context in which this verse is found indicates that even when the dilemma was the fault of the people of God, they still had hope. Hope remains alive for us, even when we fail because of our sin, because God has made a way for us to be cleansed. Once we repent, we are placed in right standing with God again, and He would not appreciate our enemies mocking us.

Sometimes, unbelievers make mockery of the church, pointing to Christians who are weak and seem to be less "righteous" than some "good" sinners. However, an imperfect Christian is in better shape than a good person who has no relationship with God. It is not our good works that make the difference. It is the faithfulness of God to care for His own. When we stand before God, the question is not, "How good have you been?" The question is, "What have you done with Jesus?" God resists the proud and gives grace to the humble.

Let us never be dismayed when the world laughs over the state of the church. We will arise. Even when it seems dark because we have gone astray, God will shine the light of His Word upon us and guide us back to the right place. We must never give up.

I will look to God for encouragement if I stumble or fall, because He loves me and His mercy endures forever. I will be encouraged when I see failure in the church, remembering that God will never leave us. We are His people, and He will rebuke, chasten and restore.

Day 173
Romans 14:12

"So then every one of us shall give account of himself to God."

In Romans 14, Paul gave instructions to the church about how to get along with each other and be respectful of the conscience of other believers. He encouraged them to be humble about their convictions on various issues, realizing that a man has to ultimately answer to God, and not his brother. He urged them to refrain from being a stumbling block to other believers, who were uncomfortable doing what they felt freedom to do.

It is important that we remind ourselves of our accountability to God. Our behavior should constantly reflect that awareness. Sometimes, we are tempted to make decisions that will make relatives or friends happy, even though we are uncomfortable in our hearts. It is possible to act in a way we feel will bring us favor with someone who can help us get ahead in some way, although it goes against our conscience. Not only are we tempted to do what pleases others, but in a society that is flooded with humanism, it is possible to struggle with self satisfaction. In other words, we can become selfish and think only of what makes us happy, regardless of what God thinks about it.

Let us be quick to remind ourselves that it is before God, and not a mirror, that we will stand in judgment. We will not only face God in the end, but every day as well, as He hears our prayers and determines our promotions or demotions. Our Father resists the proud and gives grace to the humble. If our good works will stand the fiery test, they must be God's works, and not just things we did for God.

I will examine and adjust my attitude about accountability regularly. I repent of all deeds I have done to please myself or anyone else above God. I will live in such a way that I will always be unashamed to stand before God.

Day 174
Micah 7:7

"Therefore I will look unto the Lord; I will wait for the God of my salvation: my God will hear me."

What a beautiful statement in Micah 7:7. The prophet speaks of the confidence God's people can have in Him. It does not matter what the circumstances appear to be. We can exercise patience, because God hears and responds to all His children who call on Him in faith. That is absolutely special.

A songwriter wrote, "Because He lives, I can face tomorrow." The key is not just the fact that Jesus is alive, but that He also loves us and is actively involved in our lives. If He would give His life for us, what will He not do for our benefit while we serve Him? Paul said in Romans 8:32, "He that spared not his own Son, but delivered him up for us all, how shall he not with him also freely give us all things?"

It is essential that we remain aware of our divine connection. It will bring us peace and comfort in pleasant and unpleasant times. Let us thank the Lord today for the blessed assurance that He never leaves or forsakes us, and always listens to and responds to us.

I will look to God, my salvation. I will wait for Him. He always hears me.

Day 175
Jude 20

"But ye, beloved, building up yourselves on your most holy faith, praying in the Holy Ghost"

Praying in the Holy Ghost, or praying in other tongues, as the Holy Spirit gives the utterance, charges us up. It strengthens our spirits and helps us resist temptation. It produces boldness and enables us to do things that will amaze us.

Speaking in other tongues, according to some former Satan worshippers, is terrifying to the enemy. The devil fights against the manifestation of being baptized with the Holy Spirit, because it confuses him, and he hates what it does for us. Even in communist countries where they have tolerated churches to a small extent, those who spoke with other tongues were absolutely forbidden. Even the godless knew that the Christians who were baptized with the Holy Spirit were more powerful than those who were not. They knew what Jesus prophesied in Acts 1:8 "Ye shall receive power, after that the Holy Ghost is come upon you."

When we receive the ability to pray in a heavenly language, Satan fights to stop us from using it. He finds candidates who will try to convince us that the whole business is crazy, or those who will degrade it in some other way. Just because someone is filled with the Holy Spirit and speaks with tongues does not make them perfect. It is up to each of us to take advantage of, and use properly, everything God gives us. Speaking with tongues is one of many things God has made available to us to help us win in the game of life. When used in conjunction with other things, such as walking in the fruit of the spirit, regular praying in the spirit can make us powerful and effective ambassadors of Christ. Among other benefits, it increases our ability to hear from God accurately.

Let us stir up the gift within us and begin now, this moment, to pray in the spirit. Jude tells us that we build up ourselves on our faith. It takes faith to pray in a language we have not learned. We must lift up our voices and trust the Holy Spirit for each word. This is a way we exercise our faith. Exercising faith is good, because it is practicing dependence on God.

I will stir up the gift in me and pray in other tongues more. I will build myself up on my faith, praying with the Holy Spirit's help.

Day 176
Deuteronomy 7:9

"Know therefore that the Lord thy God, He is God, the faithful God, which keepeth covenant and mercy with them that love Him and keep His commandments to a thousand generations.

What a comfort to know we have a God we can trust fully. His Word is eternally dependable.

Deuteronomy 7:9 shows us that God's mercy can be extended to someone a thousand years after His Word has been spoken. That explains His mercy and favor upon the modern descendants of Abraham, Isaac and Jacob, despite the fact that many of them are not serving Him. Proverbs 11:21 says the seed of the righteous shall be delivered. No matter how Satan has tried to wipe out Israel, it has been impossible, because of a covenant God made with their forefathers thousands of years ago. The suffering they have experienced is a result of their own wrongdoing, but the mighty deliverance that has come to them is not to their credit. The supernatural has taken place to bring them victory, all because of a faithful God.

Sometimes we look at people and wonder why they are still alive, or why they seem to have so many chances. We think maybe someone is praying for them. That is possible. It is also possible that they are reaping the rewards of a great great great great grandparent who had a covenant relationship with God.

David once searched for a descendant of his deceased friend, Jonathan, to show favor to because of a covenant they had between each other. When he found Jonathan's descendant, he did not check to see if he was good enough. The only qualification the man had was that he was a descendant of Jonathan. That caused David to show him special favor. That gives us insight into the power of a covenant, the way God's people understood it.

We can experience divine favor through utterly no credit of our own. (We can also establish a flow of divine favor for our descendants, because of our relationship with God.) Apart from our natural blood line, we have a spiritual blood line that constantly causes us favor. The Bible says in Galatians 3 that we are Abraham's seed through Jesus Christ. Romans 8 says we are children of God and therefore heirs and joint-heirs with Christ.

That should bring us to a point of great humility. If we have ever thought we must be all right because God has shown us favor, we may want to think again. We may need to correct many areas, but we can still experience the favor of God, because of <u>His</u> faithfulness.

I humble myself before God, who has shown me undeserved favor. I am more thankful for His grace. I will endeavor to live in such a way that my children will also be blessed through my obedience.

Day 177
II Chronicles 16:12-13

"And Asa in the thirty and ninth year of his reign was diseased in his feet, until his disease was exceeding great: yet in his disease he sought not to the Lord, but to the physicians. And Asa slept with this fathers, and died in the one and fortieth year of his reign."

What an indictment against a king of Israel! He relied totally on physicians, instead of God. God is not against medical professionals who use the talents He gave them to help hurting human beings. He is, however, against our using them as substitutes for Him.

Doctors should be viewed as people to whom God has given skills to help humanity. We should never choose between God or doctors. Our total reliance must be in the Lord, and we should see the doctor as a vessel Our Father can use to help us. All our help comes from the Lord, whether natural or supernatural. It is obvious that supernatural power to help comes from God, but all natural talents and abilities also come from Him.

I will rely on God as the source of my total supply. Whether my help comes from natural or supernatural means, I will thank God, who gives every good and perfect gift.

Day 178
II Chronicles 32:7,8

"Be strong and courageous, be not afraid nor dismayed for the king of Assyria, nor for all the multitude that is with him: for there be more with us than with him: With

him is the arm of flesh: but with us the Lord our God to help us, and to fight our battles. And the people rested themselves upon the words of Hezekiah King of Judah."

Whose words carry the most weight with us? That is an important question we must ask ourselves. The answer reveals the kind of relationship we have with God and the level of faith we walk in. The passage above says the people rested themselves upon the words of Hezekiah, king of Judah. Regardless of what may have come to their minds or what others may have said, they chose to accept the words of the king as most reliable. Thus, their behavior was one of rest, or confidence.

Jeremiah 17:5 tells us that a man brings a curse on himself by departing from the Lord in his heart and putting his trust in man, or making flesh his arm. We can tell where our confidence is when we react to circumstances. For example, if we were to go to the doctor and he gave us a bad report, would we fall apart as though his word were the most reliable – the word we would rest ourselves on? What about the banker, the realtor, the judge, or any other official? If we act as though a man's word is the final one, we are relying on flesh. We must always see what God has to say about the subject and let His Word be the last thing we say about the matter.

God's last word for those who trust Him is always victory. That does not mean everything will be rosy or without trouble, hardship or heartache. It simply means that if we keep our confidence in Him, respecting Him as final authority, He will take even tragedy and turn it into triumph. It means sad moments may occur during our story, but there will always be a happy ending.

God's Word is my word to rest on. I will look to the Lord, who is my shepherd, for the final word in every situation.

Day 179
Matthew 10:24

"The disciple is not above his master, nor the servant above his lord."

In Matthew 10, Jesus sent His disciples out to minister on His behalf. He gave them instructions on what to carry and how to conduct themselves. He warned them about unpleasant things they might encounter. When He described the persecution they would face, He told them that whatever men had done, or would do to Him, they would also do to them, and even worse. Verse 25 of this same chapter says, "It is enough for the disciple that he be as his master, and the servant as his lord. If they have called the master of the house Beelzebub, how much more shall they call them of his household?"

We expect to endure persecution. We are not supposed to allow anything to discourage us from our mission as ambassadors for Christ. He is to be our example of enduring suffering and staying committed. It may seem simple. Yet, it is something we must ponder from time to time. The way many Christians react to difficulty shows we are still not prepared to handle challenges to our faith and commitment. Understanding thoroughly what Jesus taught about persecution will lead us to a life of consistency in endurance and obedience.

From time to time, we have done things that were against the still small voice in our spirits. It was the gratification of our flesh that motivated us to make the wrong move. The disciple moved out of position and put himself above his Lord, who was attempting to guide him through his inner man. When the negative consequences came along, we reacted, saying something like, "OOPS! I missed it again. That was not unnecessary. If I had only followed my spirit, I could have avoided that blunder."

So, let us ponder Matthew 10:24 today. We can endure more than we have already endured. We have not suffered as much as our master. It is in our power to be consistently obedient, as we use the tools God has given us. Among those tools are prayer, Bible study, meditation and regular confession of the Word out of a spirit of agreement with God.

I am submitted to my master and Lord, Jesus Christ. I will be a good ambassador of Christ, as I allow the Holy Spirit to help me. I can endure and overcome anything that comes my way, through Christ who strengthens me. I am obedient.

Day 180
Matthew 15:14

"Let them alone: they be blind leaders of the blind. And if the blind lead the blind, both shall fall into the ditch."

It is the willfully blind who Jesus was referring to in Matthew 15:14, when He said, "Let them alone." What a horrible state to be in - left alone. That is the consequence of those who refuse to see. When we do not understand, God pursues getting insight to us. However, we are accountable for the enlightenment we do receive. If we refuse to act upon what we know, we will be permitted to "fall in the ditch." It behooves us to be doers, and not hearers only.

Apart from grasping this warning for ourselves, we can also use what Jesus said to help guide us in our pursuit to get truth to others. As sowers, we must continue to plant the seeds God has given us. It is a temptation sometimes to stay with the seed that falls on stony, thorny or wayside ground. We try to force the unreceptive ground to encompass our seed and begin the fruit-bearing process. However, while we are exerting energy on the wrong soil, other good soil candidates are waiting for seed. It is important to learn when to "let them alone." Jesus wanted everyone to receive and be blessed. He even wept over the city of Jerusalem, because He wanted so much for them to receive what God had planned for them. In Matthew 23:37, Jesus said, "O Jerusalem, Jerusalem, thou that killest the prophets, and stonest them which are sent unto thee, how often would I have gathered thy children together, even as a hen gathereth her chickens under her wings, and ye would not!" Nevertheless, He realized that every man must make his own choice, and God respects the choices we make, no matter how much He wishes they would be different.

So, let us do two things. First, let us make sure we do not become ditch victims, by refusing to do what we know is right. Secondly, let us respect the choices of others, and allow the Holy Spirit to guide us, when it is time to move on to other ground with our seed basket.

I will practice following the Lord completely. I will fall into ditches less and less, as I increase more and more in obedience. I will respect the choices of others, as I continue to sow the precious Word of God to those I am able to reach.

For a complete list of tapes and other materials by Marilyn Gool please write:

Conquerors Publishing
P.O. Box 240433
Charlotte, NC 28224